The HECHT EFFECT

For Athletes... For Coaches... For Life

Steve Hecht

MW01593940

The Hecht Effect
Copyright © 2011 by Steve Hecht

All rights reserved. No part of this book may be reproduced or transmitted in any form or by any means without written permission from the author.

ISBN 978-0-9725150-1-6

Cover by Dennis McLain
Printed in the USA

Dedication

To Laura,
My wife and best friend.
Thank you for helping me to remain true to my passion for
helping people. You are a true champion and the finest
person I have ever known.

To Cole and Ciera
You are the best kids I could ever ask for.
Thank you for sacrificing so much time with Dad, while I
have been gone for the season, and working on this book.
I love you guys, and I am so proud of both of you!

Acknowledgments

Much of the information that I share in this book comes from my experiences as both a professional baseball player and a Major League Coach. In over 30 years of involvement in amateur and professional sports, I have had the privilege of working with some of the best coaches, players, and athletes in the world. The inspiration for this book stems from my constant curiosity regarding what allows athletes to excel, and what sets the best apart from the rest. I have had the unique opportunity of taking this curiosity to various sports, locker rooms, batting cages, bullpens and dugouts as a player and as a Performance Coach. I have been privileged to be a part of helping talented players become the best in the world; while I have been equally privileged to be a part of their personal and professional lives. I have grown professionally and personally as a result of these friendships.

First of all, I wish to thank my wife for working so hard and for persevering for long hours, to help get this manuscript completed; and my two children – Cole and Ciera. Your unconditional love and support allowed me to write this book.

Thank you to my Father-in-Law and Mother-in-Law, Pat and Connie Norton for all of your hard work and support. Your faith in me has helped bring this project to fruition.

To my family: Mom, Jaime, Julie and Stacy for always encouraging me to do this.

To Bill Weingartner, the smartest person I have ever met. Thank you for your friendship, and for taking the time to review this book and offer your invaluable insight.

Thank you to the many coaches I have had the privilege of talking to, learning from, and working with. To name a few:

Rick Adair, Mike Brumley, Ty Van Burkleo, Dom Chiti, Alan Cockrell, Duane Espy, Rudy Jaramillo, Buck Showalter, Tony Taylor, Lee Tinsley, Don Wakamatsu and Ron Washington.

Thanks to the hundreds of amateur and minor league players for their willingness to discuss their performance successes and challenges.

Finally, I would like to offer a special thank you to some of the following Major League players that I have had the pleasure of working with. I am grateful for the time that we worked together, which often allowed me to learn with you, and from you. David Aardsma, Erik Bedard, Adrian Beltre, Russell Branyan, Jamie Burke, Marlon Byrd, Nelson Cruz, Chris Davis, Doug Fister, Ken Griffey Jr., Franklin Gutierrez, Josh Hamilton, Matt Harrison, Felix Hernandez, Eric Hurley, Rob Johnson, Shawn Kelley, Ian Kinsler, Brandon League, Cliff Lee, Jose Lopez, Mark Lowe, David Murphy, Brandon Morrow, Carlos Silva, Sammy Sosa, Ichiro Suzuki, Mike Sweeney, Matt Tuiasosopo, Jason Vargas, Jarrod Washburn, Sean White, C.J. Wilson, Chris Woodward, Jamey Wright, Michael Young and so many others… Thank you.

About the Author

Steve Hecht is a former professional baseball player, and has coached in the Major Leagues with the Texas Rangers and Seattle Mariners. As a Sport Performance Coach, he has worked with numerous Major League and minor league coaches and players, as well as professionals and amateurs from a variety of sports. Steve enjoys instructing coaches, athletes and teams at every level, and teaches them specific skills relevant to their sport.

Steve was drafted out of high school by the Pittsburgh Pirates in the 13th round, but declined the offer and chose instead to play at the Division I collegiate level. Drafted again in the 5th round in 1987 by the San Francisco Giants, he played 9 years of professional baseball. In 1987 he was honored to be a part of the USA Pan-American Baseball Team, and proud to be a part of their silver medal victory.

Steve has a Bachelor's degree in Psychology, an MA in Management, and is currently pursuing a PhD. in Health Psychology and Behavioral Medicine. He also enjoys consulting in Organizational Training and Development, and has authored and published the successful online personality assessment *www.careerfitter.com*. He is married with two children, and resides in the Dallas-Fort Worth Metroplex.

The Science Behind *The Hecht Effect*

"The problems of tomorrow will not be solved by the thinking of today"

-- Albert Einstein

Firstly, everything we do is based on our understanding of applied psychology and neuroscience. Hating complexity ourselves, we have tried to simplify the existing science into something useful by sharing our understanding of it. Science without solutions is however a pointless pursuit, so this is the value we hope we have added: what to do, when you think you can do nothing as a coach, a trainer, a mentor.

The Hecht Effect is a solution-based application for improving performance. Its ongoing goal is to offer emotional relief by removing obstacles and empowering others to perform at a higher level. Resolving this emotional disruption in performance is the reason for *The Hecht Effect.*

Dr. Roy Sugarman

Director, Applied Neuroscience

Dr. Roy Sugarman is the Director of Applied Neuroscience at Athletes' Performance. Dr. Sugarman is a clinical neuropsychologist, a clinical psychologist, and an internationally-recognized expert in optimizing brain performance. Using state-of-the-art measures of brain output, Dr. Sugarman determines what underpins the personal and unique success of an athlete. To read more of the science behind *The Hecht Effect*, please go to www.thehechteffect.com and read the *Foreword* by Dr. Sugarman.

8

Contents

Toolboxes

All Truth Goes Through Three Steps:
First, it is ridiculed. Second, it is
violently opposed. Finally, it is
accepted as self-evident.
–Arthur Schopenhauer

Introduction

Come to the edge.
We might fall.
Come to the edge.
It's too high!
Come to the edge!
And they came,
And we pushed,
And they flew.
—Christopher Logue

Athletes know from experience, that when they feel tense, anxious, and unsettled, they perform well below their ability. The purpose of this book is to provide athletes and coaches with powerful tools for greater athletic performances. These tools have been developed and established for, and by, coaches and athletes. When you read this book, you will immediately think more clearly and feel better about what you do. Athletes and coaches who consistently use these simple tools and techniques experience significant performance advantages. Each chapter provides insights and simple approaches to improving athletic performances. These tools help athletes and coaches learn *how* to enhance performance, while the *why* becomes secondary to results.

The mind and emotions are an athlete's closest ally, or fiercest enemy. Athletes and coaches that become masters over their mind and emotions can more easily become masters in athletic performance and coaching, all too often the tools that are missing from an athlete's and coach's toolbox are mental and emotional. Athletes and coaches unknowingly disrupt their own success due to not having mental and emotional tools. The mind and emotions can undermine the best physical preparation and plan.

An athlete must understand that no amount of physical preparation and planning can consistently overcome a busy mind and anxious emotions. In order for athletes and coaches to have ongoing success, they must have *simple tools* to deal with the mental and emotional demands of competition. There is increasing success for athletes and coaches who learn to command their minds and emotions. Emotional success quiets the mind and maximizes physical tools, talent, and hard work. It allows athletes to perform at a higher level with less effort.

This book will change the way you play, coach, and view sports. Emotional success equips athletes and coaches to better handle success and failure. This in turn, positions them for better results. Emotional success does not come through better mechanics; it comes from greater understanding. Emotional success brings a feeling of power beyond words. It allows players and coaches to enjoy competition and maintain perspective. The most powerful achievement an athlete can experience is emotional success. More muscle, more mechanics, and more hard work are secondary.

This book will provide athletes and coaches the tools they need to bridge the gap between mechanics, thought, and emotion. These tools will help you maintain confidence, concentration, and composure in practice and competition. You do not need to take my word for it, just start reading and experience greater mental and emotional success.

Chapter One
THE EMOTIONAL GAME OF BASEBALL

The game of baseball is played physically, learned mentally, and succeeded at emotionally. –Steve Hecht

The game of baseball is an EMOTIONAL game! It is succeeded at emotionally. Sports are an emotional event. Unfortunately, the mechanics of the game have been taught as the primary focus. From Little League to the Major Leagues, mechanics are taught as the primary focus for baseball success. While *fundamentals are vitally important*, this limited approach undermines achievement and success more than most players and coaches understand.

To be clear, good mechanics are foundational to a player's development, but they are **not** the most important factor to ongoing success. The game of baseball is about quieting the mind by winning the emotional game. Win the emotional game, and you are better positioned for baseball success. Lose the emotional game, and baseball is the most difficult and frustrating endeavor in sports or life.

To the point, too much emotion can overcome the strongest body and best mechanics. Too little emotion can cause a player to feel and play flat. Emotions break down mechanics, concentration, and focus more often than competition does.

Emotions break down mechanics, concentration, and focus more often than competition.

For example: When a hitter is uncomfortable hitting with two strikes or has a fear of striking out, he actually undergoes "emotional spikes." Emotional spikes cause tension in the body, slow down reaction time, and hinder a batter's ability to recognize pitches. With this mindset, a hitter may try to hit a pitch early in the count to avoid the uneasy feeling a two-strike count creates. The hitter learns to dislike hitting with two strikes, because the feelings of fear and anxiety associated with it are miserable. The hitter wants to avoid this uneasy feeling, so he swings at pitches early in the count; which in reality cuts down his strikes and pitches per at-bat. All the batting practice and hard work is short-circuited by the more powerful emotional tension that results from wanting to avoid a two-strike count. The batter programs his own mind to avoid two strike counts at all costs, even if it means swinging at a less favorable pitch early in the count, and being a .260 hitter instead of a .300 hitter. Hitting with two strikes ends up taking the fun out of hitting, and leaves the hitter with an ongoing sense of emotional unrest. The emotional unrest created from hitting with two strikes ends up defining the hitter. He is overly anxious to hit early in the count, and even more anxious if he has to hit with two strikes. *This is emotional unrest*! Emotional unrest deserves the relief of what I refer to as *emotional success*.

If a player is not enjoying emotional success, then he is likely dealing with emotional unrest. Emotional unrest causes a player's mind to be overly active. The greater the emotional unrest, the more active the mind becomes. A player wants to feel relief and have a quiet mind, but he has been trained to seek and find relief through mechanical adjustments. Well-meaning coaches and parents want to help their players, so they "over-coach" and share more information than players need or can handle. The athlete's mind is further cluttered and distrusting, all

16

stemming from the player and coaches trying to "fix" what is wrong.

On the other hand, the more **emotional success** players enjoy, the quieter their minds and emotions become. Emotional success allows athletes to trust in their mechanical preparation and ability. Emotional success is the avenue to a quiet mind. The quieter the mind and calmer the emotions become, the greater the chances are that the athlete will benefit from his hard work and mechanical training during competition.

WHAT IS EMOTION?

Emotion is based in three words: "energy-in-motion." When energy is no longer in motion, it gets stuck in the body and creates tension and difficulty for the athlete. During competition most players can feel emotion get stuck in their stomach, chest, neck, legs, or shoulders. Emotion is real. It has mass, or it would not be felt in the body. Emotion stops in the body when the mind is fearful, anxious, excited, etc... Athletes can easily become aware of *where* their emotion gets stuck, by thinking about how they feel in game situations.

Feeling emotion flow through the body is natural and necessary for the athlete, but feeling emotion stop in the body is *not*! When excess emotion is stuck in the body it creates tension and is based in fear, doubt and/or distrust of one's abilities. Given the same situation, the athlete that allows emotion to flow receives the benefit of greater awareness, quicker reactions, better decision making, and better physical performance.

When a coach's mind is quiet, he communicates trust and confidence more effectively. He will make better decisions according to the situation-at-hand and have a better understanding of his players. The coach with a quiet mind sees what others do not and accurately responds to the moment. Coaches with quiet minds stay in the moment and have creative insights for keeping their players in the moment.

The quieter the mind of a coach, the more likely the player will enjoy his experience, having more energy and focus for the game. When a player feels concerned about having to deal with emotional outbursts or verbal assaults from coaches (or parents), he is robbed of complete concentration and becomes less productive. He is not emotionally free. Coaches (and parents) that want to communicate trust and confidence in their players will make huge strides when they quiet their own minds before interacting with players. When a coach's mind is quiet, he is more insightful and aware of what the players need. Sometimes it may be a word of encouragement, a "kick in the pants," or an understanding silence. To be clear, an understanding silence carries a feeling of reassurance, while a punitive silence carries a feeling of disappointment and judgment. All of these approaches communicate something different to players.

Hard work is most beneficial when it is trusted. When coaches trust in their players, the players sense it and are positively affected by how they feel. A trusting coach will always receive a better long term pay-off by communicating trust and confidence. As a coach, be willing to *ask* what you can do to best communicate trust and confidence. The greater the level of trust and confidence players and coaches have, the greater the enjoyment and chance of success. The quieter the mind and emotions are, the easier it is to:

- Get into the rhythm and flow of the game.
- Slow the game down.
- Be creative with adjustments.

As an illustration: Imagine a river flowing downward. When an athlete is "flowing," his mind is quiet, he breathes correctly, has little tension, and the game seems to slow down. When a player is "flowing" in competition, this is how it happens:

EMOTIONS →

　　THOUGHTS →

　　　　MECHANICS

Release the emotion, quiet the mind, and allow the body and mechanics to perform correctly.

Teaching mechanics to improve thought, and calm the emotions, is like swimming upstream. Athletes and coaches can learn to bridge the gap that exists between mechanics, thoughts, and emotions. All three must work together to maximize performance success. Well-meaning coaches do not need to keep swimming upstream if they will utilize the tools available.

TOOLBOX

The Maui Method

Take a breath and think of an emotion you would like to dissolve. Feel that emotion in your body. Now lay down on the beach in your mind, and let that emotion drift away.

Imagine yourself in Maui, Hawaii. The temperature is a sunny 82 degrees. You are lying on the beach with your eyes closed, and the breeze off the ocean is keeping your body temperature perfectly comfortable. You have a cool drink and a good book to read, for as long as you can stay awake to read it. You feel the salt water gently spray you and smell the food being prepared for the evening luau. Seagulls are sounding off as the waves continue to rhythmically ebb and flow.

You are now so relaxed that you cannot tell the difference between consciousness and unconsciousness. At this moment you are totally aware that you have everything you need. Life has never been better. Everything is exactly the way it should be…

The Athlete's Anthem

Perfect Clarity

I see my objective with flawless clarity.
The image in my mind is perfect.
My eyes are intensely focused and trusting.
My thoughts and emotions are assured.
My vision is fixed on the prize.
I have perfect clarity.
My emotions are calm.
I am at peace. —Steve Hecht

Chapter Two

Performance Number

You cannot teach a man anything; you can only help him to find it within himself. –Galileo

What is YOUR number? I am not asking about the number on your jersey. I want to know your performance number. One of the first things I try to establish with a player is his performance number (this can be done for coaches as well). An athlete's performance number rests somewhere between 1 and 100, and it reflects a feeling of maximum rhythm, power, and timing with minimal effort.

An athlete's mental and emotional intensity determines his physical intensity. The performance number represents the level of mental and emotional intensity an athlete feels in practice or competition. For example, one All-star outfielder and AL MVP told me he hits best around a performance number of "70." An All-star infielder told me he feels that when his performance number rests around "60" (mental and emotional intensity), he is best physically prepared to hit.

When an athlete's mental and emotional intensity is too high, the body reacts more slowly and is filled with excess tension and anxiety–which decreases peak performance. If an athlete's mental and emotional intensity is too low, the body does not adequately respond to the demands of practice and competition. Awareness of the performance number allows an athlete to assess if his mental and emotional intensity is helping or hurting his performance.

An athlete's performance number is affected by how his body feels and how active his mind and emotions are. Adjusting the performance number (mental and emotional intensity) up or down helps an athlete prepare for competition and directly affects his performance success.

An athlete's performance number is fueled by emotion, and best directed by a quiet mind. Anxious emotions and thoughts move an athlete further from his ideal performance number, while calm emotions and single-minded trust move him closer. An athlete performs best when he has awareness without thought, and this happens when his physical movements are free from excessive emotions. Athletes who learn to consistently master mental and emotional intensity by maintaining their performance number will compete at their best more often. *A performance number is a feeling that athletes learn to relax into.*

For example, I discussed the performance number with a Major League relief pitcher who has over 10 years of experience at the Major League level. He said he maintained the best command of his pitches when he was around "80." Then, I asked him what his performance number was when the phone in the bullpen rang, and he was told to get ready. He told me that when the phone rang his mental and emotional intensity went directly to "100." His excitement for competition fueled his emotions well past his ideal number of 80. So, this pitcher knows his best command rests at 80, but he admitted he very often enters the game and throws many crucial pitches at an intensity of 90 to 100, which lessens his chances of pitch command and consistency.

An interesting principle that came out of that conversation: **Athletes do what they need to do, in order to get to a comfortable emotional level.** What that means is simply this:

sometimes a pitcher may end up giving up a 3-run homer in the process of trying to get back to the comfort of his ideal performance number. In other words, it is important to learn how to get to your performance number, before competition begins.

Remember, emotions (especially under pressure) are much more powerful than the best physical planning and preparation. Coaches, be aware of this pattern in your players, and arm yourselves with the tools that work best for them. Athletes perform with a pattern consistent with their performance number, and their mechanics are most often an expression of that number.

This is why so many players perform well in practice, and often fail to perform the same way when the game begins. The further a player is from his performance number, the less consistent his mechanics will be. Game situations naturally increase mental and emotional intensity. So, it is vital for an athlete to use tools that lower his pre-game performance number, because adrenaline will naturally increase intensity.

To help find your performance number, read the definition below and slowly *feel* the meaning of the words.

Your performance number is felt when *you*:

Are trusting, are non-striving, are non-needing, are not seeking validation, believe before you see results, know what to do without thought, are powerful but not forceful, are timely but do not rush, achieve without indulging in the feeling of achievement, adjust to the needs of the moment, have singular focus and complete awareness, do not resist what is, accept that everything is exactly the way it should be, are creatively disciplined and entirely unshakeable.

What is your number today? **50**

As an athlete, you will have your greatest chance at success by staying as close to your performance number as possible. Your unique timing, rhythm and power are reflections of your performance number. That timing, rhythm, and power will flow unhindered when your body feels electric and your mind and emotions are quietly and confidently supporting the body's demands.

If your performance number gets too high (emotional spiking), your mind is overly active, your body tenses up and your performance declines. If your performance number gets too low, chances are, you will be unprepared for competition. If your body feels electric and your mind is at ease, you can more easily adjust to the demands of competition. When your mind is at ease, your body will feel more energized and electric/responsive. Your daily performance number reveals whether your mind and emotions are overly active or supportive. Focusing on the number is not nearly as important as knowing what the number feels like and having definite ways of getting to it.

Keep in mind that a college linebacker at a performance number of "80," a big-league relief pitcher performing at "80," and a golfer performing at 80, will look very different due to the demands of the sport and the personality competing.

Each day, be aware of your performance number. Make it a point to let emotion go, and never expect yesterday's thoughts and emotions to carry you through today's competition. If you want to flow in competition, let thought and emotion go moment to moment. This is the way you will learn to perform at your best.

TOOLBOX

Capture Today's Performance Number

Picture and feel yourself sitting in a high performance race car. The car and the engine represent all the hard work and training you have put into preparing for competition. As you sit behind the wheel, you start the car and imagine yourself driving around an oval-shaped race track. You are the only one on the track. Your car can go over 200 miles per hour, but you always warm your car up by driving it at 1 mile per hour. You drive around the track at 1 mph for as many laps as you need until your mind and emotions are moving at 1 mph.

No matter how many laps it takes, you do not accelerate until your mind, breathing, and emotions are moving at 1 mph. When your mind, breathing, and emotions are moving at 1 mph, you start to accelerate. The car responds, and you feel the momentum, power, and precision pulsating through your body. This is the point where most athletes lose their performance number and get caught up in the speed and excitement of the moment. They spike emotionally, but not you. This is the point you set yourself apart as an athlete.

When you are driving this car, you realize a strange thing happens. You recognize that as you push on the gas pedal and go faster around the track, your mind and breathing get slower, you get more focused and aware. All of the exhaust and noise going out of the car is left behind. The exhaust represents your emotions, and the noise represents your thoughts or "mind chatter."

The harder the engine works, the more emotion you release. The faster the car goes, the slower your mind and breathing get. Keep letting go of emotion, and trust your ability and preparation. You are now going around the track at over 200 mph, but your mind, breathing, and emotions are unshakeable. They are working in perfect unison with your body. You are physically electric, and your mind and emotions are quiet and focused. You have just captured your performance number.

The Athlete's Anthem

I am trusting, content, and approved. I do not need or seek validation. I believe before I see results. I know what to do without thought. I am powerful but not forceful. I am timely but I do not rush. I achieve without indulging in achievement. I adjust to the needs of the moment. I have singular focus and complete awareness. I do not resist what is. I accept that everything is exactly the way it should be. I am creatively disciplined, and entirely unshakeable.

–Steve Hecht

Chapter Three

TRUST

A person who doubts himself is like a man who would enlist in the ranks of his enemies and bear arms against himself. –Alexander Dumas

Trust is defined as believing in what you do, and *feeling* the conviction to do it. The trusting athlete relies on his character, ability, and strength to compete. One American League All-Star infielder told me his success comes largely because he *trusts* his swing and ability more than other players. He said there are more physically talented players in the minor leagues, but he believes he is successful because he trusts his ability and approach more than they do. He stated, "If the mechanics of my swing are good enough to get 4 hits one day, then why would I doubt my swing and ability on the days that I don't get a hit." I asked him when was the last time he thought about the mechanics of his swing, and he said he was probably 11 or 12 years old.

An athlete learns to trust himself by putting himself in situations in which he has no control. If an athlete cannot successfully handle the emotions of failure, he cannot completely trust his mechanics and abilities. Many different thoughts and emotions are experienced in competition that cause an athlete to stop trusting his approach and ability, but the *trusting athlete* has learned how *inefficient* mechanical thought really is. Trust is not mechanical. Trust is conviction. Trust is not a feeling, but it definitely has a feel to it. The more an athlete thinks about his mechanics, the less trust he feels. A measure of distrust is always found in mechanical thought. The completely trusting athlete is free from grinding mechanical thoughts because he trusts his preparation and approach. Searching for trust through mechanical adjustments is a trap players fall into. This approach is like trying to keep a hot air balloon in the air while the balloon has a tear in it. The balloon can be kept in the air, but it is very inefficient, and it takes much more hot air (energy) to do so.

When a player learns to surrender to trust, he finds it easier to abandon mechanical thought. Trying to constantly figure things out is exchanged for trusting what he knows. He is no longer caught up in trying to discover trust, he has found it. He has realized that trusting in who he is and what he does is the only highly productive use of his time and energy. The distrusting athlete struggles in the quicksand of his own mechanical thought and doubt as he continues to sink. The trusting athlete ends the struggle by believing and trusting that he is enough. Why would a player want to spend too much time in mechanical thought, when it creates a feeling of distrust and a lack of confidence? Coaches should read the previous sentence again and think about how much mechanical thought is necessary for each player. Constant mechanical instructions are the loudest form of distrust an athlete can receive from a coach. Athletes, your mechanical thoughts are the loudest form of distrust you can communicate to yourself. Chasing trust through mechanical adjustments naturally leads an athlete to wonder and ask, "What day will my mechanics be good enough?" which is *distrusting*. Granted, ***good mechanics are foundational to development***, but what day are the mechanics of a hitter's swing, or a pitcher's delivery, *good enough*?

If certain mechanical adjustments work well one day, then why are we told to try something else another day? Are we getting poor results? Mechanical difficulties can often be resolved by resolving difficulties in thought and emotion. The level of trust and conviction a player has can often be seen in his mechanics. *The outward mechanics are an expression of the inward thoughts and emotions.*

Many well-intentioned coaches get frustrated telling players the same mechanical thing over and over. This frustration comes from trying to resolve a more powerful thought or emotion through mechanical adjustments, or trying to coach from the outside in. Making mechanical adjustments is the most common coaching approach to subduing the "beasts" of doubt, fear, and anxiety. However, these beasts CANNOT be permanently overcome through mere mechanical adjustments. The more mechanical an athlete's thoughts become, the less trust he experiences.

Mechanical thoughts during competition come from wanting and striving for a feeling other than trust. The problem is a player wants to feel better (more confident), so he starts tinkering with his mechanics in order to find a better feeling. This begins an insane cycle of chasing a better feeling by chasing a different or "better" mechanical adjustment. However, what if he approached the "problem" differently? What if he became a master of letting go of the feeling that is communicating distrust and a lack of confidence? What might happen if he *first* learned to let go of the feelings communicating distrust before he practiced or played? What if he gave himself permission to feel better on purpose? What if he ended the trust versus distrust struggle that comes from chasing the "magic pill" of mechanics?

What is the point of taking so many swings, or throwing so many pitches if you are not going to invest the time to trust what you have practiced? *Trust* is an investment players can make in themselves. Coaches, the quicker you can help a player release mechanical thoughts and feelings of distrust, the easier he will make adjustments, and the sooner he will *trust*! There is no natural obstacle that keeps an athlete from experiencing trust. It is concealed by the manufactured emotions of fear, doubt, and anxiety. You will be able to sense trust *now*, if you just let go of those unproductive emotions.

Learning Trust during a Game of Catch

This exercise is used for baseball, but it can easily be adapted to any sport with a little creativity. Simply, select a skill that is easily performed by the athlete(s). The skill must be simple enough to do successfully without thought or anxiety. The athlete that learns to trust his abilities is positioned for maximizing his performance.

Let's begin teaching the feeling of trust through a game of catch. The more difficult a skill is, the more trust is necessary for success. Trust allows the task to be accomplished more easily. Your ability to relax reflects your willingness to trust. One of the first exercises baseball players perform after stretching is playing a game of catch. Early on, and with proper coaching, baseball players find they can play a game of catch without anxiety or thinking.

Coaches and players must learn to recognize the value of trust in one activity so that it can be transferred to others. Once simple tasks are regularly accomplished with ease, the focus should shift to how the athlete feels while performing the task.

The sense of trust, the breathing, the speed of the movement, should be captured by the athlete. Then the same mental and emotional intensity can be transferred to the next, more difficult skill.

For example, a baseball player is able to play a game of catch without thought or anxiety, catching 100 balls in a row. At a point, he should stop the game of catch and reach down to pick up a bat, while maintaining the same mental and emotional feeling and intensity established during the game of catch. If the trusting mindset and feeling captured during the game of catch is duplicated when the bat is picked up, then performance anxiety is lessened and a more trusting mindset is established. The player now successfully hits 100 consecutive baseballs.

Interestingly, the majority of baseball players will say that the moment they pick up a bat, their minds get active and they start thinking about mechanics. Mechanical thought is not trusting. Capture the feeling of trust in the simplest athletic drills, so that players can recognize and transfer the same feeling to practice and competition. The greatest performers learn to trust their mechanics.

Another example comes from golf. A professional golfer told me he is very effective hitting his tee shots consistently down the middle of the fairway. His body language is confident and trusting when he speaks of his ability to use his driver. However, when discussing his putting he feels doubt and anxiety. He has a keen awareness of the feelings he has associated with both his driver and his putter.

Now, he captures the trusting feeling he has with his driver and transfers it to the putting green. Consistent repetitions while feeling trust with his driver teach him trust while putting.

Too often, there is a natural tendency to carry anxious and unsure feelings from one skill, at-bat, swing, game, etc., to

31

another. For example, a batter strikes out and the at-bat is over, but instead of concentrating on the current moment and letting go of any emotional attachment to the previous at-bat, the batter continues to re-run it in his mind. This builds up negativity and emotional distress in his body, which creates tension and anxiety for the next at-bat.

Sometimes an athlete will trust his ability to play defense and distrust his ability to produce offensively. The same trusting mindset and emotional feelings that allow him to excel on defense are not transferred to offense. This type of player will typically trust on defense and *think about his mechanics* on offense.

At times an athlete learns to compartmentalize so well, that he keeps his positive and trusting feelings alive in one area and disconnected in another. His positive and trusting approach in one performance area is prohibited from carrying over into other areas. In fact, it is more common to see the negative and distrusting struggles from one area spill over and contaminate other performance areas. When a player learns what trust feels like, breathes like, and moves like, he can allow it to consistently permeate every other aspect of his athletic preparation and performance.

TOOLBOX

Get in the Pool of Trust

You can feel trust now, if you will commit to letting go of any thoughts or emotions that cover it up. Go through each sentence as slowly as you like, and pause after each sentence as long as you feel like it.

Trust is here...

Take a few deep breaths and let them out slowly...

Imagine you are quietly sitting on the edge of a beautiful swimming pool...

The water temperature is perfect...

Put your feet in the water and continue breathing slowly as though time does not exist...

Feel the water in the pool drawing out all your fear, anxiety, stress and doubt...

Let all your thoughts and emotions get drawn out through your feet and dissolve in the water...

These thoughts and emotions want to be dissolved if you will let them go... let all of them go...

Continue letting go as long as you like...

Now, enjoy the powerful feelings of calm, trust and confidence...

Embrace calm, trust, and confidence...

You are ready to get in and swim in the pool of trust...

Be thankful for what you have. Be thankful for what you are, you have it all... Now play and live with trust...

The Athlete's Anthem

Trust is the freedom to succeed or fail. Trust has no concern for the past or the future. Trust calms my mind and emotions. Trust is the courage that maximizes my ability. Trust creates focus. Trust patiently waits for expression. Confidence is the expression of trust. I trust. I am confident. I am the perfect expression of trusting confidence. –Steve Hecht

Chapter Four
THE ATHLETE'S "FEELING"

We know too much and feel too little. At least we feel too little of those creative emotions from which a good life springs. –Bertrand Russell

The athlete's "feeling" achieves maximum impact, with minimal effort, at just the right time. Athletes are constantly working to find a "feeling," *the feeling.* They know this *feeling* will serve them well in competition. **This *feeling* is the mental calm and physical intensity that gives them the confidence, trust, and focus, which allows them to perform at their very best.** Athletes work hard to capture this *feeling,* and they often find it difficult to hang onto.

Instead of the athlete relaxing *into* the feeling and enjoying it, he wants to control it and maintain it, which only re-creates the starting point for tension and anxiety. Athletes want to find *the feeling,* and they get more anxious the longer it escapes them. Even when they capture the feeling, they start to experience a sense of fear at the thought of losing it. In either case, the athlete finds both a sense of calm with *the feeling,* and a sense of anxiety at the thought of losing it.

They confidently know the feeling will give them an edge, but they also worry about how long it will last. This is one of the many disruptions that exist inside an athlete's mind. Every day it uses up huge amounts of an athlete's energy, while waiting to be resolved. How can an athlete expect to perform at his very best

35

when energy is being wasted? Energy is being used to search for *the feeling* that is already there.

This *feeling* is experienced by an athlete when emotions like fear, doubt, and anxiety are let go. *The feeling*, is **always** present within an athlete, but it is often covered up by some level of anxiety, frustration, fear, anger, or disappointment. ***The feeling is concealed from an athlete, because the emotions behind fear and doubt are greater than the emotions that lead to trust and confidence.***

Ironically, most athletes believe in the importance of the mental and emotional approach, but they seldom invest time in it. Instead, athletes work harder physically, or spend more time trying to figure things out; but they fail to recognize the cause for losing *the feeling* in the first place.

If an athlete will consistently let go of excess emotion, he will find it much easier to uncover *the feeling* that promotes his success. It is not necessary to focus on why the emotions exist, but it is necessary to learn how to let them go. Remember, if you do not have *the feeling* you want for competition, it is because there is another emotion that is overshadowing it.

The most common approach to finding *the feeling* for athletes is by doing more physical activity, or creating a new mechanical adjustment. Unfortunately, this approach can be hit or miss. If it were possible to always find it by doing extra physical work, then more athletes would consistently perform with *the feeling*. Some days a certain physical routine relaxes the mind and uncovers *the feeling*, while other days it does not. It never seems to be totally under the athlete's control. Naturally, this causes anxiety. The athlete then feels the need to start physical activity hoping to find out if *the feeling* is there for today's competition. If the mind is tense, the physical performance will be less than it should be. We must understand that the feeling is *always* there, but fear, distrust, and anxiety are concealing it. *If emotion is released before beginning the physical routine, the athlete will have a much easier time finding the feeling and experiencing its benefits.* The common athletic mantra seems to be, work harder and harder and hopefully today *the feeling* will show up.

For example, hitters taking batting practice will often search for *the feeling* in the midst of the activity. They enter the cage with anxiety, and hope that if they hit enough baseballs, the anxiety will go away and *the feeling* will show up.

If a hitter doesn't realize that emotions like frustration, fear, and distrust have covered up *the feeling*, he will end up taking more and more swings trying to rediscover it. He is not sure how many good swings it will take to make him less anxious, but "one more" or "a couple more," can turn into 8 or 10 more *anxiety swings*.

This type of batting practice session is not productive. The hitter's purpose is to find *the feeling*, but unknowingly he is trying to burn excess emotional energy created by anxiety, frustration, fear, and distrust. This type of batting practice is really a search for mental and emotional trust.

This process is inconsistent and unpredictable for the hitter, which can cause more anxiety. As a result, the hitter tinkers with his swing so that he can capture a feeling he *thinks* he needs for that day's competition. This approach is literally hit or miss, and most often changes from pitch to pitch, at-bat to at-bat, or game to game.

As an example, in my three seasons with the Texas Rangers, Michael Young never once came out early for batting practice. Likewise, in my two seasons with the Seattle Mariners, Ichiro Suzuki never came out for early batting practice. In fact, I asked Ichiro if he had ever taken early batting practice, and his answer was, "No." Both players are All-Star performers, and both players *trust* in what they do to find *the feeling*; and it is seldom to never mechanical.

Thought and emotion dictate physical movement. Athletes must understand that mental and emotional mastery provides the best opportunity for peak performance. If an athlete will prepare his mind and emotions before physical activity, everything else can happen with less effort and more efficiency.

Athletes want *the feeling,* and all the benefits that come from having it; but they will seldom take the most efficient path to uncovering it. Establishing mental and emotional routines takes very little daily time and effort, but strangely it is avoided or overlooked. Some athletes are not sure what to do, some are too lazy to do it, and others are simply afraid of becoming more than they are. Most devoted athletes will not hesitate to put in an extra hour of *physical* effort in search of *the feeling*. Yet, the same athletes could not imagine making the same commitment to an extra hour of *mental or emotional* preparation.

As an athlete, what would happen if you committed yourself to put in 5 minutes of mental and emotional preparation, for every hour of physical preparation? The benefits would be felt immediately, building a lasting foundation for ongoing success. Try it for 2 or 3 days and find out for yourself. For every hour of physical effort, allow yourself 5 minutes of mental and emotional preparation. Use the TOOLBOX in this book to help you. Let yourself enjoy the benefits from making this commitment.

TOOLBOX

Approve of Yourself

One of the most powerful emotional tools an athlete or coach can give himself is approval. Sit back and relax. With each breath you take, allow yourself to feel waves of approval for no reason whatsoever. Just sit and approve of yourself. Approve of everything you think about yourself. Imagine the ocean waves represent your feelings of approval. Each wave coming to shore delivers all the approval you can handle. It never ends. Wave after wave of approval soaks through you. Be completely comfortable basking in approval. Now dive into the water and submerge yourself in approval. Swim in approval, and learn to give yourself approval all the time, for no reason at all...

The Athlete's Anthem

Life is good... The power that mightily works within me is life. It is my life. It does not flinch. It does not fear. This power in me is grounded in absolute goodness. This power grows and increases as I flow in it. All power and all confidence stems from my unshakeable belief in the perfection of my uniqueness. Uniqueness is good. It is perfect, so I do not have to be. I rest in the knowledge that all goodness resides inside me. I am an athlete of supreme certainty, and unmatched conviction... –Steve Hecht

Chapter Five

The Trusting Athlete

In all activities of life, the secret of efficiency lies in an ability to combine two seemingly incompatible states: a state of maximum activity and a state of maximum relaxation. –Aldous Huxley

An athlete performing with *feeling* will always outperform an athlete performing with *thought*. Thought conceals feeling. Increasing thought decreases feeling. Less thought, more feeling. More positive feelings lead to more success. A player's feelings always reflect his thoughts. A player's ongoing feelings about his swing or pitch delivery will largely determine his success or failure. When an athlete knows how he wants to feel, he can learn to develop and maintain this feeling through a consistent mental, emotional and physical routine. Poor thought, or too much thought, will conceal or cover up the feelings necessary for consistent and ongoing athletic success.

In competition and pressure situations, athletes must understand that emotion and over thinking will break down mechanics. Mechanics become more consistent and efficient when *feeling* is not hindered by *thought*. Erratic thoughts, feelings, and emotions make athletic consistency and performance very difficult. Erratic thoughts, feelings, and emotions require excessive energy to restore and maintain peak performance levels. The greater the emotional peak or valley a player has, the more energy it takes to return to emotional stability and physical ease.

If coaches do not understand how to create the thoughts and feelings that best support a player's performance, then they become another obstacle to the player's performance. In these cases, it takes a very unique player to ignore or overcome the uneasy feelings created by an anxious coach or parent.

If a player's good feelings are a determining factor to his success, then why do most coaches spend the majority of their time investing in coaching techniques that primarily support thinking? Many coaches get so consumed with teaching mechanics that they lose sight of the athlete's most important performance factor; *how he feels*. Does teaching mechanics create clarity or confusion? Does it promote trust or distrust?

I have found there are two types of athletes; *trusting* and *distrusting*! **Trusting athletes play to win. Distrusting athletes play not to lose.** Trusting athletes act on what they know. Distrusting athletes continually collect more information and avoid committing to anything consistently. Distrusting athletes are constantly tinkering with their mechanics.

Likewise, I have found there are two types of teams; trusting and distrusting! Trusting teams play to win. Distrusting teams play not to lose. Trusting teams have players that trust each other to act on what they know to be best for the team. Distrusting teams continually collect more information and avoid committing to their teammates or a style of play.

Distrusting teams are constantly searching for an identity. They are constantly tinkering with their players and plan, which keeps them from establishing a foundation to build upon. Trusting teams build their approach and identity on the abilities, beliefs, and talents of the team. They maximize the talent of the group by minimizing distrust in one another.

Unfortunately, the insecure coach sometimes has his own need to feel relevant and important, which is most often satisfied by teaching what he *knows:* mechanics. Ironically, the more a coach wants to stress mechanics, the more he communicates some level of distrust.

The coach that teaches and communicates trust through his body language, tone of voice, and verbal content, will find that mechanics becomes a smaller percentage of his coaching routine. In fact, the more a coach finds himself teaching mechanics, the more thought and distrust he communicates to his players. The trusting players learn how to perform well, by believing in what they know works best for them. This is covered in more detail in chapter 19, "The Coach's Corner."

The coach or player that spends too much time seeking a better mechanical way to do things, or the mechanical "magic pill," may be feeding his own need to feel better about himself; but he is only creating doubt, confusion, and distrust in his players. Well-meaning coaches most often do this innocently. They want to help players get better, but often don't know how; or they fail to recognize the best way to do it. An important question to ask any player: What do you want to feel in order to perform at your very best?

Now coach, ask yourself, "Do I help players think, or do I help players feel? Do I know how to help them feel what they need to?" As a coach, are you willing to ask a player if you are helping him feel what allows him to perform at his best, or do you more often add to his thoughts? Again, an athlete performing with *feeling* will always outperform an athlete performing with too much *thought.* If you want to know if you are a "next level" coach then ask yourself this question, "Can I help a player improve his performance without discussing anything related to mechanics?"

43

The answer to this question for most coaches is, "NO!" However, if you become a master of helping players feel trusting and confident, you will position yourself as a *next level* coach; truly unique and set apart. Likewise, if a player becomes a master of helping himself feel trusting and confident, he will position himself to be a *next level* athlete. When *feel* is restored, physical ability is maximized.

Every emotion carries a thought with it. When emotion is let go, thought goes with it. Athletes that let emotion go, let thought go; and they quiet their minds.

Cy Young award winner Felix Hernandez is the best example I have seen of consistently performing with feeling in an absence of excess thought. No doubt Felix Hernandez is highly talented, but he was a .500 pitcher for the first few years of his career. This story has been told many times, but Felix became a *next level* pitcher after he responded to a challenge that Manager Don Wakamatsu gave him. The challenge was for Felix to take control of his emotions, and pay closer attention to opposing base stealers. Equally as important, Pitching Coach Rick Adair built a relationship with Felix and was able to make him aware of how his emotional spikes during a game broke down his mechanics and caused him to lose command. Felix responded to emotional coaching and has become one of the most dominant pitchers in the world. He understands the importance of pitching with *feel,* and, interestingly, it is nearly impossible to engage him in a conversation about mechanics.

Emotions demand expression. Let emotions go and you are free from their demands. –Steve Hecht

TOOLBOX

Be Still

Find a quiet place so you can be still for a few minutes. Take a deep breath, and imagine pouring all your thoughts and emotions into the ocean. You are an athlete. Let go and trust yourself. When you slow your mind and emotions down, you allow your preparation and training to take over. Your body feels at ease. Continue to imagine pouring all of your thoughts and emotions into the ocean and realize everything is being put into perfect order.

Your mind is quiet. Now quietly say out loud "BE" and pause for as long as you want before saying "STILL." The pause **between** the words is where performance excellence is found. Your emotions are free, you feel lighter and your mind is quiet... every pitch, every inning, and every game.

BE... STILL...

It's up to you. Now, enjoy the power of peace from being still...

BE... STILL...

The Athlete's Anthem

There is nothing as magnificent as the beauty of this moment. I do not need to do anything or be anything other than myself. I am by myself, but I am not alone. I have presence. I am aware of this presence inside me. It is magnificent. –Steve Hecht

Chapter Six

TRUE CONFIDENCE

What lies behind us and what lies before us are tiny matters compared to what lies within us.
–Ralph Waldo Emerson

A good performance, or a poor performance, often defines an athlete's self-confidence. The self-confidence trap is like a bank account. Good performances are like deposits in the account, while poor performances are like withdrawals from the account. This is a common outlook in the sports world. Players, coaches, fans, media, and family members help you keep track of your self-confidence bank account. They will give you deposits of praise for good performances and make withdrawals of criticism for poor performances. Often times, and unfortunately, poor performances are given more emphasis than good performances. The value is placed on the withdrawal and not the deposit. With this mindset, it doesn't take long before a few poor performances have an athlete overdrawn in their self-confidence bank account, and this is the self-confidence trap.

When an athlete understands the self-confidence trap, he can avoid it. Self-confidence is a great ally when it is on your side; and a heartless enemy when it is not. It is a brutal task-master when it is based in results. Self-confidence based in results is *not* true confidence. True self-confidence believes and trusts *before* seeing results, even when results are not ideal. When an athlete learns to let go of any thought or emotion that covers up self-confidence, he moves closer to true self-confidence. Fear and doubt are like emotional blankets that cover up self-confidence.

Victory or defeat does not define self-confidence. True self-confidence always moves forward. It is the power to create what you believe already exists. True self-confidence does not chase approval or accolades. It is not subject to change, because it is grounded in an unshakeable belief that you are enough at this moment. True self-confidence is based in a belief that produces results. It achieves, without being absorbed in the achievement. True self-confidence does not seek praise, it seeks expression. True self-confidence is not arrogant. It says, "I am comfortable with myself, and I believe in what I do."

TOOLBOX

Dissolve

Confidence is present in the absence of fear. Imagine fear, doubt, or any other thought or emotion being like antacid tablets dropped into the ocean. Just keep dissolving your emotions in the ocean water until calm and courage surface. Fear wants to be dissolved. Doubt wants to be dissolved. Let them have their way...Keep dissolving any emotion that covers up your confidence...Dissolve them all...

The Athlete's Anthem

The belief that I have in myself is unwavering. I can never have too much confidence, respect, and success for myself. I cannot believe and achieve too much, because I am an expression of God's genius. All of my talents, gifts, and abilities are the result of His handiwork. My self-confidence comes from understanding that I am created in His perfect design. That alone puts me in step with the rhythm of my life. I believe in my uniqueness. My athletic career and life are a demonstration of my confidence in action. So, I think big of myself, I think well of myself, and I think it again and again.

–Steve Hecht

Chapter Seven
THE THOUGHT-FULL ATHLETE

To the mind that is still, the whole universe
surrenders. –Lao Tzu

Athletes *do not* have difficulty because they cannot think, but because they cannot stop thinking. Athletes are fooled into believing that they cannot effectively compete without thinking. Thought produces a very low form of competition. The high performing athlete performs unhindered by thought, and he cannot perform at his highest level when ruled by thought.

Thought is tricky. It sets out to serve the athlete, with the full intention of taking over. It desires to enslave an athlete and control performance; and it prevents the mind and body from working together. Unending thought wastes energy and creates tension in an athlete's body.

In time, over-thinking creates an insecure feeling in an athlete. He stops trusting his abilities and starts trusting his thoughts, and he continues to return to the well of thought when a lack of confidence and trust leave him thirsty. Athletes think that in order to improve performance, they must do more thinking. Unfortunately, at this point they have created a belief that thoughts are essential to their athletic success. Trusting in thought takes over for trusting in ability.

Too often, athletes make a habit of using thoughts to cope with their daily dose of uncertainty. If an athlete has been trained and coached to only improve performance through mechanical adjustments, then they live on a merry-go-round of thought and mechanics. To illustrate, merry-go-rounds are full of energy and music and often create good feelings while riding on them, but you always end up back where you started. Merry-go-rounds and mechanical thought have one major thing in common. They offer a temporary distraction from reality. Merry-go-rounds make kids feel joy and distract adults from the moment. Thinking becomes a merry-go-round of distraction, which keeps athletes from dealing with the mental and emotional unrest that calls for another mechanical adjustment. Mechanical thought gives athletes something new to think about in an effort to feel better, but it ultimately leaves them back where they started.

As an athlete makes a mechanical adjustment in search of relief from self-doubt, the adjustment temporarily disrupts the feeling of self-doubt, and seems to promise lasting relief. The athlete may feel, or say, that the new adjustment is the "magic pill" he has been looking for his whole career; only to find a short time later, that self-doubt has resurfaced, and a new mechanical adjustment is required. Mechanical adjustments are often nothing more than a way to disrupt, or distract from, the black hole of self-doubt.

Self-doubt is cyclical. An athlete's temporary sense of relief will eventually be disintegrated by the more powerful feeling of self-doubt. Self-doubt starts and ends at the same place: a *feeling* that something is not quite right and needs to be adjusted. Unfortunately, the most common adjustments for eliminating the feelings of self-doubt are mechanical. Tinkering with mechanics enables an athlete's "factory of thought" to create something new and start the merry-go-round of self-doubt.

Thoughts cover up *the feeling* an athlete longs for, and the athlete is deceived into believing that *more* thinking will uncover that "magic pill" of clarity and focus. This type of over-thinking can keep an athlete in a state of desperation and survival.

Coaches share their best thoughts, in the hope of improving athletic performance. They talk *at* an athlete, and in turn, the athlete talks *at* himself. The athlete is convinced he will figure it out if he keeps grinding out more thoughts. This is a cycle that drains energy from an athlete until it eventually wears him down and takes over. *Thought takes on a life of its own!* Some athletes and coaches may lie down at night and be unable to sleep, because their thought factory will not shut down. Athletes, you *do not* play sports to be a problem solver! You play to be a performer. Sports are not a problem, but too often athletes and coaches think and feel as though they are.

At times, athletes may feel they are sitting in the passenger seat, while their thoughts are driving the car. From the passenger seat, the athlete tries to convince his thoughts to surrender the wheel. However, those thoughts are able to convince the athlete that the car is best operated while *they* are driving. The athlete gets tired of arguing with his thoughts, and eventually lets them have complete control. Ultimately, the athlete surrenders the enjoyment and peace of mind that comes naturally from not thinking, in order to feed the thought factory, instead of simply trusting.

The Difficulty of Thought and Performance

Did You Ever Stop to Think, and Forget to Start Again? –A. A. Milne

The primary challenge with over-thinking is that it is mostly concerned with what has happened, or what will happen.

Thought has little use for the here and now. It wants to dominate and consume every facet of an athlete's performance and life, and when continually fed, it will do so. Given enough time and attention, an athlete can no longer differentiate himself from his thoughts.

Athletes find they are constantly having to remind themselves of what they *used to feel like,* or encourage themselves with the hope for a better *feeling* next time. An athlete believes that a good performance will finally quiet his thoughts; however, this is a great deception. A good performance will only bring temporary relief.

Relief from thought is silence, but thought and silence cannot coexist. Silence is natural and perfectly content without thought, but too much thinking can cause an athlete to be uncomfortable in silence. So, when an athlete or coach is uncomfortable in silence, they may be over-thinkers.

Constant thinking cannot consistently provide the athlete with the here and now focus that is required to perform at the highest level. Over-thinking causes an athlete to go too fast or too slow. Thought has very little rhythm of its own because it is constantly searching for ways to satisfy the past and the future at the same time.

Too much thinking will cause a dancer to move awkwardly to the rhythm of the music. When dancers allow the rhythm of the music to freely flow through them, they are outwardly expressing freedom from thought and performing in the here and now.

Athletes are most creative and insightful during periods of quiet and inner stillness. In quiet moments and stillness, athletes discover that they can have complete awareness without thought. Creative and insightful athletic performances occur in the absence of thought.

54

A high performing athlete has a quiet mind during competition. An underperforming athlete has an overactive mind. A high performing athlete discovers his creativity in silence. A *thought-full* athlete constantly searches for more information and continually generates more thoughts.

Emotion and Thought

Emotion is a reflection of thoughts. If you cannot currently define what you are feeling, it is because your thoughts are suppressing it. Ask yourself, "What am I feeling?", and silently wait until the answer surfaces.

An underperforming athlete is defined by low thoughts like doubt and distrust, as well as low emotions like fear and anxiety. Yet, neither consistently disrupts the high performing athlete. Excessive thinking uses energy that should be reserved for focusing and performing.

TOOLBOX

The Shark Tank

This metaphor has been used successfully to help athletes in a variety of sports and will immediately help the *thought-full* athlete in competition.

Imagine a huge open shark tank full of water and sharks. Now imagine a gymnast's balance beam running from one side of the tank to the other. Imagine climbing a ladder up to the beam in preparation for walking to the other side of the tank. The sharks are about 12 inches below the narrow balance beam you are about to walk on. They are swimming aggressively around you, and they are hungry.

Your heart and mind start racing, and fear causes your body to start tensing up. You have practiced walking across the same beam over an *empty* shark tank for years. Your coach has helped you refine your form and body position for the best possible style and balance, but now the sharks are in the water and this time it's "for real." It's game time!

As anxiety starts to increase, the well-meaning coach says to the athlete, "Breathe, and remember to put one foot in front of the other just like we practiced. You can do it, just don't look down at the sharks and get distracted. Stay focused on what you are doing, and you will make it to the other side." This coaching approach is very mechanical, well-intentioned, and very common. Coaches give what they know to give: information and encouragement.

Let me explain this common scenario. The athlete and coach prepare all season for the goal of competition. In this case, getting to the other side of the shark tank is the goal. During practice, everything is similar to the actual performance: the length and width of the balance beam, and the tank height and depth. Everything is similar except that the sharks are not in the tank during practice. When the athlete steps out onto the balance beam, there are crowds of people in the stands and the cameras are rolling. Friends and family members have come to watch, and the coach uses his bull horn to shout out instructions and encouragement. Thoughts and emotions get stirred up, and then the athlete begins to walk across the beam with extra tension and anxiety. The athlete knows how to walk across the beam, but now excessive thoughts and emotions disrupt his rhythm, and take over as his guide. All the while, emotion starts to grow stronger and more out of control. The athlete's performance number is too high, and the simplest task of walking across the beam becomes difficult. Let's address what is going on for this athlete:

1. The coach has the best of intentions but shouts out instructions that prompt the athlete to begin thinking about his mechanics. The coach innocently clutters the athlete's mind with instructions that create unproductive emotions.
2. The athlete has worked hard to perfect his mechanics but does not entirely trust his mechanics because of fear and doubt. He wants to please his coach, parents, and fans so he *thinks* through the performance.
3. The athlete's form represents the physical mechanics the coach feels responsible for. The performance reflects on him.
4. The sharks represent all the thoughts in the athlete's head. The more sharks, the more thoughts an athlete has.
5. The water in the tank represents all the emotion in the athlete's body.

Now, the most *common* way of getting across the tank is to practice enough, so that *hopefully* all will go well at game time.

The coach is responsible for helping to make sure that the mechanics of the performance go well. The athlete often feels responsible for pleasing the coach by thinking through the mechanics. The sport psychologist wants to talk about the sharks and determine how they got there and how the athlete needs to breathe and concentrate on what he can control.

STOP! What if you made it simpler?

It's game time. You do not care about mechanics right now; you do not care about pleasing your coach; you do not care to discuss the many hungry sharks (thoughts), how they got there, or how they make you feel. YOU ONLY CARE ABOUT DRAINING THE SHARK TANK! Climb down off the ladder. Go to the bottom of the shark tank and open the powerful valve that releases all the water (emotional) pressure. Imagine that all of the emotion in your body is like the water being drained out of the tank.

Just let it go... Keep letting the water drain out of the tank as long as you are competing. You will find that when you drain the water (emotion) out of the tank (body), the sharks (thoughts) die, and the body is more prepared to compete. Thoughts cannot live without emotion, like sharks cannot live without water. Release the emotion and the thoughts will die as the mind gets quiet. Drain the water out of the shark tank, and the sharks will die.

Drain the emotion from the body and discover how much easier it is to freely flow and walk across the balance beam without thought. *Excessive thinking is not necessary for the prepared athlete.* Emotion that is stuck in the athlete's body is unproductive. It must continuously flow through the athlete to make performance consistently successful.

Whether you are stepping into the batter's box, onto a pitcher's mound, a golf course, a football field, a basketball court, a soccer field, or any other field of competition, try draining the shark tank of emotion before, during, and after competition. Allow yourself to be completely in the moment of competition. Now, literally imagine that your emotion is the water in the shark tank that is being drained from the huge valve of emotional relief. Emotion flows out of your body like the water in the shark tank. Keep your mind free of thought by letting emotion leave your body.

You will feel lighter and freer because your imagination is being used constructively. If you feel less weighted down and anxious, it is working. Notice how much easier it is to perform. It is much easier to compete when your mind is quiet and your emotions are flowing. If you drain the shark tank continuously, the positive emotions that enhance performance will continue to increase, while the negative emotions that hinder performance fade away.

The Athlete's Anthem

Peace and power know when to speed up and slow down. Peace and power are never in a hurry. When I step with my left foot, I feel peace. When I step with my right foot, I feel power. Peace and power are the foundation for my performance. They are always present within me. Peace and power regulate my every breath. I am in step with peace and in rhythm with power. I feel peace and I compete with power. My peace is extraordinary. My power is relentless.

–Steve Hecht

Chapter Eight
The Fear of Success & Failure

Each time we face our fear, we gain strength, courage, and confidence in the doing. −unknown

The following activities will assist an athlete to identify and release fear. Athletic competition is the very best manner by which an athlete is revealed to himself. Competition can, and often does, reveal hidden fears in an athlete. Athletes can try to hide their fears, but competition has a way of unveiling what is on the inside. Most of society can often avoid confronting their fears, but athletes have the opportunity to meet them head-on through competition. Whether you are a hitter, pitcher, catcher, infielder, outfielder, or any other athlete you can discover and release your fears before they show up in competition.

Hitters: Imagine *never* getting another hit. Think about at-bat after at-bat, and *never* getting another hit. No matter what adjustment you make, you never get another hit. If you start to feel emotion/energy in the form of anxiety in your stomach, chest, or throat area, etc…that is good. Allowing yourself to feel and recognize emotion allows you to release it. Imagine that the emotion you feel is like a fire burning inside you. The emotion wants to leave your body if you will let it. Now imagine opening a chimney flue and letting the smoke rise up and out. Let the emotion go, like smoke leaving a chimney. The smoke wants to escape. Just keep letting it go. Let the smoke/emotion go until the feeling inside of you weakens, and you feel lighter and freer. Let the smoke go until the fire goes out.

Again, imagine *never* getting another hit. If the feeling is weaker, you have released some of the emotion/energy associated with the fear of failure. Keep doing this exercise as often as you like in order to release any additional fear of failure. Each time you release the emotion/energy associated with *never* getting another hit, you become mentally stronger. You are letting go of the fear of failure *before* it has a chance to show up in competition.

Hitters: Imagine getting a hit *every* time you go to the plate. No one can get you out, and every swing yields another hit. If you start to feel energy in the form of anxiety or excitement in your stomach, chest, or throat area, imagine opening a pressure release valve, and let that energy escape. Just keep letting the pressure escape into thin air, until the feeling weakens and you feel lighter.

Again, imagine getting a hit *every* at-bat. If the feelings are weaker, you have released some of the energy associated with the fear of success. Try this exercise as often as you like in order to release any additional fear of success. Each time you release the energy associated with getting a hit, you become mentally stronger. You are letting go of the fear of success *before* it has a chance to show up in competition. The quiet mind of a hitter is unshaken by success or failure. The energy is released, emotional spikes are avoided, and the mind is quiet while concentration is maintained.

Pitchers: Imagine **never** throwing another strike. Think about pitch after pitch, and *never* throwing another strike. If you start to feel energy in the form of anxiety in your stomach, chest, or throat area, imagine that the emotion you feel is like a fire burning inside you. The emotion wants to leave your body if you will let it. Now imagine opening a chimney flue and letting the smoke rise up and out. Let the emotion go, like smoke leaving a chimney. The smoke wants to escape. Just keep letting it go. Let the smoke/emotion go until the feeling inside of you weakens, and you feel lighter and freer. Let the smoke go until the fire goes out.

Again, imagine *never* throwing another strike. If the feeling is weaker, you have released some of the emotion associated with the fear of failure. Repeat this exercise as often as you like in order to release any additional fear of failure. Each time you release the emotion that comes from the idea of *never* throwing another strike, you become mentally stronger. You are letting go of the fear of failure before it has a chance to show up in competition. The quiet mind of a pitcher is unshaken by success or failure. The energy is released, emotional spikes are avoided, and the mind is quiet while concentration is maintained.

Pitchers: Imagine throwing a quality strike *every* single pitch. Each pitch is another quality strike. If you start to feel energy in the form of anxiety or excitement in your stomach, chest, or throat area, imagine opening a pressure release valve, and let that energy escape. Just keep letting it go until the feeling weakens and you feel lighter.

Again, imagine throwing a quality strike *every* pitch. If the feelings of excitement and anxiety are weaker, you have released some of the emotion associated with the fear of success. Each time you release the energy associated with throwing a quality pitch, you become mentally stronger. You are releasing the fear of success before it has a chance to show up in competition. You let go of the energy and stop resisting. The energy is released, the mind is quiet, and concentration is elevated.

Infielders/Outfielders: Imagine **never** securing another ground ball or fly ball. Think about play after play you *never*

63

catch another ball. If you start to feel energy in the form of anxiety in your stomach, chest, or throat area, imagine opening your release valve, and let the energy escape. Just keep letting it go until the feeling weakens and you feel lighter.

Again, imagine *never* securing another ground ball or fly ball. If the feeling is weaker, you have released some of the energy associated with the fear of failure. Repeat this exercise as often as you like in order to release any additional fear of failure. Each time you release the energy associated with *never* catching another ball on defense, you become mentally stronger. You are confronting the fear of failure before it has a chance to show up in competition.

Infielders/Outfielders–Imagine catching *every* ball hit to you. One after another, each play is made. If you start to feel energy in the form of anxiety in your stomach, chest, or throat area, imagine opening your release valve, and let that energy escape. Just keep letting it go until the feeling weakens and you feel lighter. Again, imagine catching *every* ball. If the feeling is weaker, you have released some of the energy associated with the fear of success. Repeat this exercise as often as you like in order to release any additional fear of success. Each time you release the energy associated with catching *every* ball, you become mentally stronger. You are confronting the fear of success before it has a chance to show up in competition.

These activities are important to an athlete because they provide him a method to maintain a more consistent level of concentration, peak performance, and energy. The peak performance mindset must be supported with the right amount of emotional energy. Too little energy leads to under performance and too much energy leads to trying too hard. Rid your mind and body of excess energy by confronting and releasing the worst and best case scenarios. Your mind and emotions are then free to support peak physical performances during competition.

Your challenge as an athlete is to work hard physically and completely let go of any attachment to *results*, mentally and emotionally. Many coaches talk about not focusing on results but fail to understand the full impact of the statement. Letting go of excess thought and emotion is the very best way to stay focused on the task at hand and *not* get caught up in results. Practice releasing thought and emotion before, during, and after competition. This allows your mind and body to continually work together. Let go of emotion, and you will have quicker reactions *and* bring relief to your body. Your preparation and training will take over. A quiet mind is always productive.

EN-JOY the preparation. EN-JOY the game. When you are without fear, you are IN JOY. Are you in absence of fear? Are you IN JOY? Are you competing with an absence of fear? Completely enjoy who you are and what you do, and you will find yourself without fear. Fear will fade as your joy increases. "The joy of the Lord is my strength." Athletes who live without fear have power. Athletes who live without fear, enjoy competition.

TOOLBOX

Your Parachute

Before your next game or performance begins, imagine slowly falling to the ground with your parachute open. Slowly drift downward while looking around at how beautiful everything is. Enjoy the descent and realize how much perspective you have. From the sky, everything moves slower and seems so small. From a distance all things seem possible. Just keep drifting downward without a care or a worry in the world. Each moment you feel lighter and lighter. Keep falling towards a feeling of nothingness.

Now imagine yourself performing and competing. Notice how effortless you move, how much control you have of each movement. No stress, no strain, no problems. Now, land on your field of competition, and keep the same light feelings and perspective that you had above as your body becomes physically electric. Just let go...

The Athlete's Anthem

Moments

Moments, sobering moments in time, when joy overcomes me with blindness to anything but absolute goodness.

Moments inadequately described by words, and found beyond the experience of my feelings.

Moments when nothing exists outside the stillness of perfect calm.

Moments when neither time, nor space, can be defined by my thoughts.

Moments when God's presence staggers my steps, and stops my speech.

Moments when reality illuminates illusion; when my body and soul surrender to perfection.

Moments when knowing, and being known agree: when perfect clarity is captured, and at last I understand what it means to be free. –Steve Hecht

Chapter Nine
PERFORMANCE ROUTINES

The drop of rain maketh a hole in the stone, not by violence, but by oft falling. –Hugh Latimer

The importance of performance routines cannot be overstated. The more quality the performance routine, the more energy is available to focus and apply toward competition. The simplicity of a performance routine is just this: *it is the container that organizes an athlete's energy and focus.* An athlete without a performance routine will have inconsistent performances as a result of lost energy and focus. The absence of a performance routine will cost highly talented athletes consistency and longevity. Even the most talented athletes who lack performance routines fall short of their full-potential. Potential is wasted by using energy without focus.

Like a container with holes, so is an athlete that attempts to compete at his very best, while leaking energy and focus due to the lack of a performance routine. A performance routine makes it easier for the mind to relax, experiencing a sense of peace and calm; therefore, the athlete has more energy to focus and concentrate. Performance is more manageable when a performance routine is established and committed to. The performance routine is an anchor that keeps an athlete grounded when waves of difficulty come.

If an athlete is not getting optimal results, then his routine needs to be adjusted. A routine is foundational to the athlete's success. It provides a sense of security and keeps the mind and emotions from wandering. It may require adjustments, but it should largely stay the same when consistent performance results are being achieved. The routine should be predictably consistent, but it must contain some level of flexibility. If not, the routine then becomes a source of anxiety and stress.

Athletes need to stick as closely as possible to their routine and have a sense of resilience if something unexpectedly disrupts it. Nothing can shake the quiet mind, not even an interruption in the performance routine. If the routine is disrupted, then let the resulting emotion go. Wanting to control every aspect of the routine is unrealistic and stressful. A *complete* routine will provide awareness and recognition of the body, mind, and emotions.

Here is a simple example of the importance of performance routines: Imagine coming home from work and getting undressed. You take out your wallet and set it on the dresser; you take your keys out of your pocket and set them on the bathroom counter; you take off your glasses/sunglasses and put them on the nightstand; you put your briefcase in the kitchen; and you put your cell phone in the living room.

The next morning when you are getting ready to leave for work or school, you rush around trying to gather your things together; and waste energy searching for all of the items you scattered all over the house. As you try to remember where you put everything, you feel rushed and anxious. You get a surge of adrenaline as the time ticks away and the pain from disorganization turns into panic.

Ironically, some athletes receive some pleasure and enjoyment in feeling this emotional spike. They create their own difficulties by spreading their stuff all over the house, and then enjoy the challenge of getting everything together in order to leave on time. They are undisciplined (by spreading things all over the house), just so they can get a burst of adrenaline that makes them feel more alive and creative. Intuitively they know they are unfocused, so they let situations and circumstances occur that will cause them to refocus. This is strange for many people to grasp, but it happens all the time with professional athletes.

Players will *subconsciously* create their own challenges, like walking a batter to lead off an inning, or letting their batting average dip lower than it should, just to see if they can overcome the tight spot they have created. At the same time, they become frustrated or angry because they know in their heart and mind it did not have to be like this. They are without a routine, and they are inconsistent.

Athletes without performance routines end up looking, and playing, like they are in a hurry. They not only place their gloves, shoes, and equipment in various places, they also have their thoughts and emotions all over the place. After awhile, this seems as normal as breathing to them.

They enter competition feeling unsettled and then expect to immediately focus and concentrate on what they are doing. The absence of routine in this situation may, or may not, cost someone a game; but it does waste energy and creates an anxious feeling that makes it difficult to perform at their very best. It robs and diverts energy, while creating unnecessary panic.

Instead, try a new routine: Build a mound of focus and consistency by putting your wallet, keys, glasses/sunglasses, briefcase, and cell phone all in one location. Burn a little energy now, and have more to burn later; or burn no energy now (by putting your items anywhere and everywhere), and use a lot of energy later trying to find them. Where do you want to use your energy? It's up to you!

A performance routine helps to stop the "fight or flight" response that makes athletic performance more difficult. Competition can create the same rushed and anxious feeling that comes with trying to find your wallet, keys, or cell phone while in a hurry. A performance routine can help you avoid this panicked response.

To further illustrate, several seasons ago a young and highly talented pitching prospect had rapidly advanced through the minor leagues and quickly found himself in the Major Leagues. His first several starts at the Major League level were a struggle. So, for the next couple seasons he began the season in the minor leagues where he had success, only to be recalled to the Major Leagues and fail. Each time he failed at the Major League level he would be sent to the minor leagues, where his abundance of talent would allow him to succeed again.

Finally, one Spring Training everyone involved in his career and development had seen enough. Something had to change, and it began with addressing his performance routine. A former Major League catcher, a Major League pitching coach, and I all entered an office with this talented young pitcher, in an effort to bring an end to his Major League struggles. We asked this pitcher to return to the low minor leagues and start his career over with an established performance routine. Initially, he was so offended by our request that he asked to be released from the organization.

However, after three hours we convinced him to sign a "Contract of Commitment," and start the season in Class A baseball, three levels below the Major Leagues. Each day, it was my job to call him and check on his progress. His only mission was to develop a consistent performance routine before he could be advanced to the next level. He was asked to stay there for seven starts before advancing.

His pitching performances were not the focus. His commitment to his performance routine was. In fact, after 7 starts in Class A, he ended up 0-4 with an ERA over 7.00; however, as promised, he was advanced to the next level. He ended up 8-1 at AA and 6-1 at AAA before finishing the year 2-1 in the big leagues. Before that season ended, I was in the dugout with this pitcher and I asked him what he had learned from his experiences that year? He said, "Steve, before this season I never believed in the importance of a routine, but now I come to the field and I don't have to think; because I know exactly what I am doing." The next year he became a Major League All-Star and won 17 games.

The performance routine is the container that organizes an athlete's energy and focus.

The greatest and most highly refined performance routine I have seen belongs to Ichiro Suzuki. Ichiro is so committed and focused on his performance routine that it dictates nearly every aspect of his day. What time he eats, arrives at the field, gets dressed, stretches, swings, throws, lifts weights, etc., is all worked out in his performance routine.

Ichiro's commitment to his routine is so unwavering, that one day during the team stretch a teammate asked if he and Ichiro could take a picture together. Ichiro's reply: "Yes, of course, how about 6:06pm, because I will be dressed in uniform at 6:05." Extreme maybe, but you get the point.

TOOLBOX

Flatten Your Tires

Imagine a car that represents you as an athlete or a performer. What type of car are you? Are you a high performance race car, an off road four-wheel drive pick-up, an economy car, an electric car, etc...? Whatever type of car represents you, I want you to imagine pushing down the valve stem of each tire and deflating it. One by one, let all the air out of your tires.

Before each competition, let the air out of your tires. Allow the air in the tires to represent all of the thoughts and emotions you are getting rid of. Continue releasing all of the air from your tires until they are so flat that your car is grounded.

When your car has four flat tires, you are ready for competition. In this mental and emotional state, nothing moves you. Now, start the game with little to no air in your tires. Completely trust that you will air up your tires with the right amount of emotion at the right time to meet the demands of competition.

Some days you will need more air in your tires to go faster, and other days you will need less air in your tires to slow you down. Prepare beforehand, and trust you will know what is needed as you move into the speed of the game. You dictate the speed of the game by how much air is in your tires. Be prepared and allow the game to show you how much air is needed in your tires in order to perform best...

The Athlete's Anthem

What If?

What if my athletic career had nothing to do with me? What if all my hard work, all my gifts, talents, and abilities were meant to be given away? What if all I have done, or will ever do, is a present for others to unwrap? All the sweat, all the pain, all the trials and tribulations are for me to overcome so that others can discover the character of a winner? What if my athletic career is an opportunity to fill the hearts and minds of those in search of greatness? What if... –Steve Hecht

Chapter Ten

The Power of Commitment

If you deny yourself commitment, what can you do with your life?–Harvey Fierstein

An Athlete's definition of commitment may be: **Bravely entering a room with NO EXITS!** *Commitment is the foundation for excellence.* The moment you make a commitment to go "all in" concerning any area of your life, you begin to lower your level of stress and anxiety. True commitment brings focus into your life. It eliminates uncertainty and indecision.

Commitment creates single-mindedness and raises concentration. It brings an athlete's mind, body, and emotions into agreement. Commitment narrows thoughts and energy into a laser beam of focus, while it rids you of unnecessary distractions. For example, when an athlete makes a commitment to train his body, it brings discipline to that particular area of his daily life. When there is no commitment, an athlete is double-minded and lacks focus, which promotes confusion and doubt. Commitment often requires a higher price than many athletes and coaches are willing to pay, and it separates mediocrity from excellence. Are you committed?

In my more than 30 years of amateur and professional sports, I have never seen a better example of commitment than Ichiro Suzuki of the Seattle Mariners. His commitment to excellence in baseball is unsurpassed. During the season, he is so committed to his workouts that even on a rare off-day he will make sure someone is present at the stadium so he can work out. Whether he is in Seattle or on the road, it does not matter. Ichiro makes sure he works out and fulfills his commitment to excellence.

Once after the season ended, Ichiro was asked how many days he took off from swinging a bat. He said that he had made it through one full day, before not being able to take it any longer. After a long season, Ichiro's commitment allowed him to take only *one day* off. That type of commitment takes on a life of its own. Ichiro loves to swing a bat, and his commitment to it has allowed him to enter a room with no exits and to become one of the greatest hitters in history.

TOOLBOX

Your Room Is Ready

Imagine fully committing to some aspect of your athletic career or life. Whether it is working out regularly, practicing more regularly, or preparing mentally and emotionally. It is your choice. Fear and anxiety are the obstacles that keep athletes from committing and deciding to go all in.

Think of something you have decided to commit to, and let the past feelings of resistance rise up within you. Allow yourself to fully experience the feelings that have held you back. Now, let these feelings flow out of you like a dam opening its flood gates. All the fear and hesitation that has been trapped inside of you is being released.

Continue to let emotion go until there is no resistance left. More and more emotion is released until you feel the freedom to be yourself. Now notice how much courage you have to commit, once emotion is absent. This is the real you. You naturally possess the courage and calmness to enter a room with no exits when you release unproductive emotion. Let go of fear, and courage will overwhelm you. Inside this room you are calm, you are committed, and you are complete. Open the floodgates of emotion and flow...Just let go...

The Athlete's Anthem

I let go of every thought and emotion outside this room of commitment. Inside this room I am completely content with silence and peace. Health and happiness are restored in me. With each breath I am more calmly committed.

I fear nothing.

I want nothing.

I have everything.

I am committed.

I have no exit.

I need no exit.

I am committed.

I open the floodgates of thought and emotion, and let them run out of me... I let them flow out of me... –Steve Hecht

Chapter Eleven
The Power of Resistance

Happiness requires no effort; unhappiness requires much effort. –Steve Hecht

The feeling an athlete seeks is based in trust, confidence, calm, and quiet power. With this feeling, an athlete exudes a sincere belief in his ability to succeed. Without the feeling, an athlete will waver and hesitate. He will be tense and his movements awkward.

What keeps *the feeling* hidden from an athlete? *Resistance.* The American Heritage® Dictionary defines resistance as, "A force that tends to oppose or retard motion." Any mental, emotional, or physical barrier that obstructs the free flowing motion of athletic performance is "*Athletic Resistance.*"

Feelings are e-motion, meaning energy-in–motion. Energy, or e-motion, is *meant to be in motion* and not stuck in an athlete's body. When it stays in the body it causes tension, anxiety, and stress; and it hides *the feeling* that an athlete seeks. When this happens, it also shows up as panic, worry, sleeplessness, depression, fear, and an inability to focus and concentrate.

When an athlete is not sure how to deal with his feelings and emotions, he bottles them up, creates distractions, or vents. When he bottles up or smothers emotions like anxiety and fear, he wastes his energy trying to manage or hold onto something that should be moving. Trying to keep anxiety and fear in-check

81

wears an athlete down, because it takes a tremendous amount of energy to keep anxiety and fear under control. Fear and anxiety are not meant to be managed; they are meant to be moved and released. When an athlete is no longer able to control his anxiety and fear during competition, he underperforms or chokes.

When athletes are not sure what to do about feelings like anxiety and fear, they learn to distract themselves. Their down times are filled with listening to music, watching movies, reading, playing video games, using tobacco, drinking alcohol, or some other activity that distracts them from their restless thoughts and emotions. While all of this is done in an effort to pass the time, they are unknowingly trapping excess emotion in their bodies. Sometimes an athlete may just vent or blow up in order to move emotion. They explode verbally, or physically, in order to blow off some steam, but this is not dealing with the source of the problem. Using any, or all, of these ways to cope with emotional distress only heightens and promotes an athlete's struggle.

These approaches for dealing with emotional distress create athletic resistance. Whether you are an athlete or coach who deals with anxiety, fear, bottled up emotion, self-distraction, or outbursts, there is a better way to prepare for competition. Many times, well-meaning coaches will say, "Take a deep breath and slow down," when an athlete is unsettled or rushing. This is a good start, but it does not utilize the immense power and ability of the imagination to let go of destructive emotional energy.

During competition, an overactive mind often results in the body going into a state of fight or flight. In this state of mind, an athlete is overly anxious, tense, full of adrenaline, and not able to consistently perform at his very best. As you become a master at recognizing emotional tension within your body, mind, and emotions, you will learn that letting it go is the only effective way to deal with it. This emotional energy will *serve you*. You will no longer be *its servant*.

How to Stop Athletic Resistance

Athletic Resistance is any mental, emotional, or physical barrier that obstructs the free flowing motion of athletic performance.

Regardless of the athlete or sport, athletes have days when they do not feel 100%. Let's look at some examples: A hitter or golfer loosens up and feels like his swing is out of sync. A pitcher warms up in the bullpen and realizes he doesn't have his best fastball, breaking ball, or control. A basketball player can't hit his jump shot, or his free throw shot is off. A runner feels a step slow, or a soccer player feels out of rhythm when dribbling the ball. All of these situations happen to athletes every day, and the most natural reaction is to feel a little panic and push a little harder to get back to a "normal" performance feeling. This creates athletic resistance.

Remember that each game or performance brings its own unique feeling. Your body, mind, and emotions may not always feel like they are working together. Most days athletes have a familiar rhythm for what they do, and other days they may just feel off tempo.

Imagine that your ideal performance number is 80, but as you warm up, you feel like you are too low at 60 or too high at 100. Your mental, emotional, or physical intensity is far below or far above what you consider *optimal*. When this happens, just recognize it and remember athletic resistance is most damaging when you deny it. Whatever your performance number feels like at that time, trust yourself to relax and allow yourself to produce your best possible performance at that moment. Panicking will only create resistance, so breathe deeply and let go of any tension that rises up in you. When you realize and accept that for that moment 60 is what you have, you can free yourself to effectively execute. You will increase your chances of getting to your optimal performance number.

When you resist an emotion like fear, it becomes stronger; but when you stop resisting, it loses its strength. As an illustration, suppose fear is pushing on a door that you are trying to keep closed. Fear wants to come in, and you want to keep it out. The harder fear pushes, the harder you push back. Now, instead of pushing back and exhausting yourself, step back, open the door and let fear pass *through*. Let all the emotion of fear pass completely through. There is no need to resist it, just continue to let fear pass through until it loses all of its strength. You will become stronger and calmer as a result of not resisting.

Peak athletic performances are much easier when energy is not wasted on resistance. Let's imagine you have 3 levels to your game: gold, silver, and bronze. Everything feels and works in unison on the days you feel like gold, but a successful athlete is set apart by how he deals with the days he feels like silver or bronze. Peak performers allow themselves to trust and commit to the level they feel at that moment. Relax into the performance, and remember that part of your success is determined by how you play when you are *not* playing at your highest level.

Accept that right now you are going to compete with whatever performance level you are currently experiencing. Release all of your thoughts and emotions, until a feeling of calm surfaces; then you will find that your mind is quiet and your emotions are still.

As a practice example, allow yourself to feel a situation that creates in you some feeling of fear (athletic or personal). Now notice where the emotion/feeling shows up in your body; in your chest, neck, stomach, back, legs or shoulders. If you are not sure where you feel the emotion in your body, it may be because you have lived with this emotion so long that it has desensitized you. Just take a few deep breaths before you read the metaphor in the toolbox. You will start feeling more empowered, and at ease, as you read through it.

When you use this or any of the other methods consistently, you are training your mind to let go of emotion that should be in-motion. You will be actively letting go of mental and emotional unrest and moving closer to your ideal performance number by not resisting. When you let go of emotion, you return to a place that the mind and emotions naturally recognize as *Quiet Power*. It is a place you learn to relax INTO. It is where *the feeling* for higher athletic performance is found.

Your mind and emotions recognize Quiet Power as natural and normal. When an athlete's performance routine establishes time for Quiet Power, he maximize his physical potential and productivity. An athlete that performs with Quiet Power has more energy and more freedom to perform without resistance.

TOOLBOX

You're Welcome

Fear requires thoughts and emotion to exist. When you stop resisting any emotion, it loses its power. Let go of the struggle, and the struggle will let go of you.

If you are currently struggling with any type of slump or performance issue, stop resisting it. *Fully* accept that slumps happen. You have been aware of them your whole career. Give yourself permission to feel the emotion behind the struggle, and trust yourself to let it go. Don't suppress it, or try to manage it. Acknowledge it, and let it go. Feel this metaphor and stop resisting.

Breathe deeply as you slow down. Allow yourself to imagine a long hallway of closed doors. Each door that is closed represents an emotion you are resisting. Think of an emotion you are resisting or struggling with, and walk up to that door and open it up. Receive the feeling in, and allow yourself to let the feeling pass through. This feeling has no more power, because you no longer resist it. You openly receive it and realize how much freedom you feel. Open all the doors of resistance. You have waited your whole life to open these doors.

The Athlete's Anthem

When I have run out of things to say, and when I have run out of thoughts to think, the powerful presence within me rises up like a mighty flood and makes me aware of the greatness inside of me. I release the flood of thought and emotion and feel how complete I am. No needing. No wanting. No resistance. Just me being me... Perfectly me, all the time. –Steve Hecht

Chapter Twelve
Caught in Traffic

There is more to life than increasing its speed.
–Mahatma Gandhi

Why would a big league pitcher *try* to get stuck in traffic on the day he pitches? He pitches every 5th day, and if tonight's game started at 7:05pm he would leave his house just late enough to get caught in traffic. This pitcher has won a World Series and has had a tremendous amount of athletic success. However, he elects to drive in heavy traffic closer to 5:00, rather than arrive at the stadium at 3:00 when traffic is lighter. The flow and amount of traffic is something beyond his control, yet he still chooses to put himself among the buildup of cars on the highway and streets. He purposefully arrives at the stadium later than most, if not all, other starting pitchers. For most players/people, leaving late for a game or an appointment creates unnecessary stress and anxiety. Why would he do this?

This pitcher has learned the tremendous value of slowing down his mind and emotions before entering competition. He uses the everyday task of driving in traffic to train himself to slow down and focus on what he *can* control. He literally puts himself in a higher concentration of traffic so that he can practice slowing down his mind and emotions.

He puts himself in the "slow lane" so that he gets in rhythm with being out of control. For most people, running late in traffic and being out of control is a stress-filled event, but when your

89

mind and emotions are in a relaxed state, it is much easier to accept normal stressors like driving in traffic.

He has learned that what he does to prepare for the game is something that he can control, while what happens during the game may be beyond his control. He knows that once the ball leaves his hand he can no longer control the outcome. So, the most beneficial aspect of his success is the preparation he does before the game ever starts. In this case, his preparation begins with his drive to the stadium *in traffic*. All of this happens before he lies down to take a short nap, and then heads to the bullpen to warm-up. He has learned the value of slowing down the mind and emotions.

Let's compare driving your car, to a hitter facing a pitcher. As a hitter, you learn to respond to pitches based on what pitch is thrown in different locations. As a driver, you learn to respond to how the cars around you are moving.

As a hitter, you must stay relaxed and focused when the pitches are speeding up, slowing down, moving in and out, or up and down. As a driver, you must stay relaxed and focused when other drivers are speeding up or slowing down, swerving in and out, or not obeying the traffic laws.

As a hitter, can you stay calm and focused when the game is on the line and everyone else seems to be stressed and anxious? As a driver, can you stay calm and focused when traffic is heavy and you are running late? Is it reasonable to expect you to stay calm and focused as a hitter, when you do not stay calm and focused as a driver?

Now, let's compare driving your car to a pitcher facing a hitter. As a pitcher, you learn to get hitters off-balance by speeding the ball up, slowing it down, moving it in and out, or up and down. As a driver, you can speed your car up, or slow it down, swerve in and out of traffic, or cut others off.

As a pitcher, you can try to intimidate hitters by throwing the ball close to their body. As a driver, you can intimidate other drivers by driving too close to their bumper. As a pitcher, you can stay calm and focused on throwing quality pitches. As a driver, you can stay calm and focused on driving in an orderly manner. Do you have a difficult time controlling your mind and emotions while driving in traffic? If so, how can you expect to stay calm and focused in game situations?

If you cannot stay calm and focused while driving your car, then how can you expect to stay calm and focused when thousands of people are yelling and screaming? You can no more control the speed that someone drives their car in front of you, than you can control the speed of a pitch being thrown to you as a hitter.

Pitching is speeding a hitter up, and slowing him down, moving the ball in and out, or up and down. Hitting is staying relaxed and focused on the ball, while being ready to make adjustments to speed and location. In that regard, driving a car and hitting or pitching a baseball seem to be similar exercises both mentally and emotionally.

A Challenge to Athletes and Coaches

For years I have challenged athletes to practice mental and emotional control while driving their cars. Can someone that does not know you, and may never see you again, "throttle" your emotions or create an emotional spike in you by driving too slow, too fast, or cutting you off?

Why would you think that being calm in game situations is reasonable, when you are not able to stay calm when driving your car? If a simple drive to the stadium can disrupt your mental and emotional state, then why would you expect to have mental and emotional calm inside the stadium? The reaction to one area of life, like driving, may sometimes reveal your reactions in competition.

TOOLBOX

Your Elevator

If you feel rushed or out of control, then get on your elevator. Imagine an elevator covered with thick walls of glass moving upward. Inside the walls of this elevator thought and emotion cannot live.

You step on the elevator as it moves at your perfect speed and rhythm. There is no rushing here. Feel yourself in *perfect* rhythm with the speed of the elevator. Your elevator moves at the speed of peace. As you travel upward you leave thought and emotion outside.

Higher and higher you go, as outside thoughts and emotions disappear. You can clearly see outside the glass and notice everyone is rushing through life, as you continue to breathe and move further away from thought and emotion. Each breath puts you in perfect timing with your body and your life.

In no time at all, your elevator has put you in rhythm with your body and taken you above the clouds of heaviness. You know you are free from the burden of emotion, and completely free to enjoy this moment. You are moving at *your perfect speed,* and you know that you will get where you need to be, exactly when you need to be there. Slowly rise upward...

Now, imagine you are behind the wheel of your car..., or performing as an athlete.

The Athlete's Anthem

Nothing is more exciting than the thought of feeling my soul and spirit awaken each day, with an unbridled passion and desire to live the life of my dreams. Nothing is more exciting than to soar past the paralyzing influence of fear, and live each moment to its fullest. When clear thinking dismisses confusion, my gifts, talents, and abilities achieve my purpose. My career and life is a meaningful event, it is a living, breathing, opportunity for passion to demonstrate itself. I will set myself on fire with meaningful passion and purpose, and the whole world will show up to watch me **burn.** –Steve Hecht

Chapter Thirteen
The #1 Enemy of the Athlete

The only thing that disturbs peace is desire.
–unknown

Each athlete is unique, and each coach is unique; but there is an enemy that consistently defeats both. Athletes and coaches who understand this enemy and consistently let go of it, will be much better at playing and coaching. It's time to stop wrestling with this enemy and rediscover why you play and coach. This subtle enemy has been accepted as a normal part of sports and competition. It has been embraced and often considered essential to athletic success.

Rat Poison is 90% good corn meal and only 10% poison. Sometimes athletes and coaches get so excited about the 90% good corn meal that they forget to filter out the 10% poison that eventually defeats them. This enemy is much more dangerous, offensive, and destructive than anything else in the world of competition. The #1 Enemy of every athlete and coach is:

Wanting What You Feel You Lack!

I *have* or I *want*. Having what you want is not a problem, but wanting what you do not have is the problem. Wanting something is based in the belief that you are lacking something. "I need a hit!" is a desire brought about from a sense of lack that breeds a feeling of desperation. This is a thought process that creates performance obstacles and misery. An athlete that does not want from desperation cannot fear, is more consistent, has greater clarity, less tension, and accepts situations without changing his trusting approach.

The *want* that I am talking about is NOT the *want* that motivates and energizes the athlete. It is a desperate sense that incorrectly makes you believe that there is a void. This misguided emotion comes from a manufactured feeling of incompleteness. It breeds feelings of anxiety and stress. This type of want produces pressure because it is focused on the past or the future. For example, this type of yearning will cause a hitter to *want* a hit *before* the pitch is thrown; it will cause a pitcher to *want* a strike out *before* the ball leaves his hand; it will cause a golfer to *want* to birdie before he tees off; and it will cause a quarterback to *want* a "do-over" *after* an interception. All of these types of self-imposed demands make performing difficult.

Thought-full athletes and coaches are miserable. We are born *wanting,* and we are unconsciously conditioned from an early age to *want,* and only feel good about ourselves when we *get* what we want. We are taught that winning, happiness, and peace of mind are achieved by *wanting* and *receiving.* When you feel that you desperately need something, your mind interprets it as lack or a void because your mind thinks in pictures. Every time we experience a longing for something, our mind sees and rehearses that it must be missing. Wanting creates a deficient and insecure feeling in athletes and coaches that is never fully satisfied.

If an athlete's mind and emotions are overactive, it is the result of *wanting.* The more an athlete wants in the moment, the less his mind and emotions stay focused in the moment. An athlete cannot want in the moment and be fully in the moment. The wanting athlete creates his own problems.

96

Hitting a baseball requires complete focus on the ball. A problem begins when an athlete tries to focus on the ball and wants to get a hit at the same time. Focusing on the ball is concerned with *now*, while getting a hit is focused on the *future*. When this happens, the mind is divided, and there is a simultaneous struggle for the athlete's attention. This conflict creates anxiety for an athlete. In one moment, the athlete is filled with confidence and enthusiasm, and in the next moment a sense of doubt and low energy.

Simply put, when an athlete wants two different things at the same time, his mind is distracted. As a result, the mind of an athlete searches for a way to figure it out. This battle is so common that athletes and coaches think it is normal. It is not necessary to completely understand the conflict or unrest associated with it; it's only important to know how to silence it.

Learning to disarm the weapons that we use against ourselves is an empowering approach to performance. By doing this we can reveal the naturally quiet mind and emotions that exist inside of us. A quiet mind and calm emotions provide silence, peace, and enjoyment for competition and life.

How many times have athletes thought and coaches said, "You gotta want it. You gotta want it more than the other guy/team. If you want it bad enough, *then* you can get it." Imagine being an athlete with this mindset. You *want* success for your career, which your mind interprets as *not having* success, and then your body responds to your mind and emotions. Now you feel anxious. Notice how the feelings inside of you change just by reading the previous sentences. Not having what you want creates frustration and anxiety.

When you let go of wanting, you will be free from frustration and anxiety. Athletes and coaches live with the idea that wanting is "normal." Wanting = lacking, and living with a feeling of lack robs athletes and coaches of maximized potential and the true fulfillment of competition. Living comfortably with *want* is like the greyhound dog that chases the fake rabbit around the track. The greyhound usually never catches the rabbit, but if it does, it realizes the rabbit is phony and is seldom motivated to ever chase it again. If an athlete or coach is constantly performing in a state of lack, then all of the positive and healthy aspects of life and competition are always out of reach. Wanting will keep you chasing the rabbit in circles your entire career and life.

Wanting something is not a form of preparation, or planning. It does not allow athletes and coaches to be in the here and now. The athlete cannot *want* a quiet mind and *have* a quiet mind at the same time. He either has it or he doesn't. If you *want* to take a vacation you cannot *be* on vacation. If you *want* to go to sleep, you cannot *be* asleep. A hitter cannot *want* a hit and be totally focused on hitting the ball. When your mind thinks something is wrong or lacking, it tries to compensate by getting overly active while trying to figure out what to do to fill the void. This mind chatter causes an athlete to *press*, and it undermines peak performance. The athlete that performs with this type of mental contradiction uses large amounts of energy trying to silence it. By continually releasing any desperate desire, an athlete is able to focus and be in the moment.

*__All anxious and overactive thoughts experienced
by athletes and coaches are the result of wanting.__*

Athletes and coaches will come to realize that no amount of success or winning satisfies the cavern of insecurity created by wanting. Success may bring temporary satisfaction today, but wanting is rooted in insecurity and will be waiting to disrupt an athlete's confidence tomorrow. It creates a black hole of uncertainty that no amount of success or winning can fill, and valuable energy is wasted in this unending cycle.

After reading or hearing this, most athletes and coaches ask me, "How can I prove myself successful if I don't *want*?" The answer is rather simple: just remember that your mind and emotions do *not* work like your body. Hard work at the physical level is the greatest physical expression of what you want. The greatest expression of hard work at the mental level is focus and concentration. The greatest expression of hard work at the emotional level is peace and calm. All three are developed differently, but all three work in unison.

Hard work at the physical level is the greatest physical expression of what you want. The greatest expression of hard work at the mental level is focus and concentration. The greatest expression of hard work at the emotional level is peace and calm.

When an athlete lacks trust and confidence, he begins to want. For example, during a 9 inning baseball game a catcher will catch 120 or more pitches. If you ask the catcher how many balls he *wanted* to catch, or felt a desperate need to catch, he will tell you, "None. I just catch the ball." Without thinking or emotion he just trusts that he will catch it. Now, if you ask the same catcher what happens when he picks up a bat and puts on a helmet to hit, many times *want* begins the merry-go-round of thought and emotion, and that same trusting catcher becomes a non-trusting hitter. He must trust and allow his mind and emotions to direct his body on offense, in the same way he trusts and allows it to perform on defense. Following is a poem that correctly portrays the ill-effects of playing with an attitude of desperation or wanting.

I ONCE SAW A PITCH

I once saw a pitch that I didn't like; but I wanted a base hit
so bad that I started a fight... with myself.
I wanted to prove myself and feel okay;
So I expanded the zone and flailed away;
Before I could blink I heard "strike three;"
And the next thing I knew I had broken my tree;
I ran out to play defense with an angry jaunt, and realized
my at-bat broke down when I started to want. –Steve Hecht

TOOLBOX

The Hot Air Balloon Ride

Feel this metaphor and let go of any emotion that is bothering you. Breathe deeply as you slow down. Allow yourself to feel the emotion that you wish to let go of, like fear, anxiety, stress, etc. Now imagine getting into a hot air balloon and untying the sandbags that are holding you down. One-by-one, untie the sandbags of stress and let go of their heaviness. Cut the strings that are holding you down.

As you get rid of each sandbag, you feel yourself getting lighter and more relaxed. The sandbags that were filled with stress are untied, and you let go. Just let them go... Fill up the sandbags with emotions and thoughts, and then untie them.

When you let go of all the sandbags, you feel yourself slowly rise off the ground and begin floating away. The further you drift, the less emotion you feel. As you rise upward you allow the currents of the wind to take you wherever they blow.

You do not resist. You have no way to resist the wind. Just enjoy the light feeling that comes from letting go... Continue to rise and float away into peace and silence...

The Athlete's Anthem

I relax, trust, and believe that everything I need already exists inside of me. I no longer deny what has always been. I will stop chasing what I already have. I am completely *in* this moment. I absorb every ounce of goodness around me and I give it away. –Steve Hecht

I dare to say, *"Behold I am he. Great men have come and gone, and behold a greater now stands here where I stand, and I am that one."*–unknown

Chapter Fourteen
THE PEACE GAP

If you feel light, clear, and deeply at peace, that means the ego is conquered and you have truly surrendered. All human existence comes down to a single soul's anxious search for peace.–unknown

The peace gap exists as a result of what an athlete wants and what he has. The gap creates an underlying feeling of anxiety and stress that impedes performances. If an athlete only finds peace and happiness when he wins or performs well, then competition is always stressful. The athlete not only competes against an opponent, but when he competes for his own peace and happiness, he also competes against himself. Competition causes the athlete to constantly wrestle with how to close this peace gap.

The only way to close the gap is to surrender what you want, *or* have what you want. For instance, if peace and happiness are on one side of the gap, and good performances or wins are on the other, then the only time peace and happiness are enjoyed is with good performances or wins. In this scenario, the difficulty of sports and competition always puts peace on the other side of the divide. Athletes and coaches typically believe that they can only allow themselves to feel peace and happiness on the back of good performances and wins.

Peace and happiness are positions of strength for athletes and coaches. When peace is present, ego is absent. Ego may best be defined as: Who you think you are, and what you are going to do to prove it to the world. Ego can't coexist with peace. Athletes and coaches know ego as "the little man on your shoulder" or simply "the little man." The little man lives in your head, works from your shoulder, and whispers in your ear. He feeds on approval, longs to feel secure, and seeks to control everything. If nurtured long enough, the little man never seems to shut up or leave the athlete in peace, even when he lies down at night. The little man constantly wants something and is the source of *all* mind chatter. He promises to provide success and happiness but fully intends to dominate an athlete's thoughts, which will disrupt his physical performance and peace of mind. Peace is on one side of the gap, and the little man is on the other.

The little man's favorite job is building thick walls and prisons for athletes. An athlete will remain trapped inside his tortuous prison as long as the little man is allowed to reign as warden. The little man knows his prisoners well. He knows they cannot leave his prison as long as they continue to want what he offers. When an athlete needs to have his ego fed, he will not find contentment or peace with success. Superficial moments of satisfaction will only leave him searching for more ways to get his ego fed. The little man promises peace and happiness, but always keeps it just out of reach. We have all watched some of the most talented and successful athletes in the world fall as a result of the black hole of ego.

Your Walls

Your walls can mean safety and comfort for a time, but alone too long I think you will find that the one thing you seek, yet choose to defend, will only be found *when* your walls end. –Steve Hecht

Be thankful for what you have; let go of what the little man offers, and the prison doors will begin to open. He cannot live in the presence of an athlete that is full of gratitude and contentment. Thankfulness for this moment causes the little man to fade away and quietly release you. Right now, start reading the next TOOLBOX and allow yourself to feel calm and happiness for no reason at all. Just let go and close the peace gap because you can.

TOOLBOX

The Sky

I think about lying on an empty beach and looking into the sky on a clear day. There is no existence of time in the sky. There is no past or future. The sky does not seek anything. The sky does not resist anything. The sky allows birds to freely move through it. The sky allows everything to freely move as it wishes. I release all my thoughts and emotions into the openness of the sky. Like the sky, I enjoy limitless freedom. The sky is unending. I am unending. My peace is unending. I have a deep residing peace that continues forever...Like the sky, I am open to experiencing the freedom of unending peace.

The Athlete's Anthem

When I perform with continuous peace, I realize that everything within me is in order. I have absolute confidence and assurance because I know that all is well... –Steve Hecht

Chapter Fifteen
The Power of Music

Athletic rhythm, timing, and focus are found in a quiet mind and calm emotions. –Steve Hecht

What are you listening to? The word "music" comes from the word "muse." The definition of muse is: *to think or meditate in silence.* Music manipulates the mind to think, and it manipulates the emotions to feel. Many athletes use music as a diversion from what they are feeling or thinking, or as a way to get emotionally amped up. The music they listen to either helps them get to their performance number, or it moves them away from it. It either supports their ideal mental and emotional state, or it undermines it. Athletes are often fooled into thinking that the adrenaline rush they get from music will help them perform at their peak physical, mental, and emotional best.

Too often athletes feel that an adrenaline rush is foundational to playing well. However, the music that distracts them from their anxiety, or gets them amped up for competition, can be an obstacle to performing at their very best. Many athletes make music a part of their performance routine in an effort to think and feel differently before competition, but they fail to identify whether or not it actually improves their performance. This approach is often hit or miss. Music may help change the thoughts and emotions inside an athlete, but it may not improve his focus. When athletes rely on music as a distraction from their anxiety, they avoid dealing with the cause of the anxiety.

For example, I once worked with a hitter that had been struggling by jumping at the ball. He was a former all-star performer who had become inconsistent with his at-bats. His pre-game routine, drills, and batting practice were consistent. But when the game started and he was in the batter's box, he would get very jumpy. Naturally, when a batter jumps at something coming at him at a high speed, it cuts down his reaction time and ability to recognize pitches. The constant mantra given to him by the hitting coach was, "you need to slow down." He seemed to agree, yet he continued rushing and jumping at the ball.

I asked him about the music he listened to before the game started. He said that before the game he listened to, "the hardest, fastest acid rock he could find." He believed that getting up for competition meant getting his adrenaline going so that he could perform at his best, which actually worked against what he and the hitting coach were trying to accomplish. His music was something he enjoyed listening to. He liked the way it made him feel, but it also got his mind and emotions going too fast to perform at his best. It throttled his emotions and moved him away from his peak physical state and his performance number. The music's effect on his mind and emotions actually undermined his physical hard work and preparation. He was not able to maintain emotional consistency, so his at-bats were inconsistent. Still, he was not willing to give up his music. Unfortunately, he valued his music and the way it made him feel more than making the important adjustment of slowing down. In fact, when I asked him to define his performance number, he wasn't sure what it was. He had difficulty slowing down enough to feel, or recognize, his peak performance number. He was not willing to adjust his music, or consider that his music may have been to blame for his jumping at the ball.

I have no interest in telling any athlete what type of music to listen to. I only ask athletes to consider whether or not the emotional lift they get from their music, is improving their focus and performance. Is it providing an emotional high and a performance low? Is their music helping or hindering their hard work and preparation? If an athlete performs best at a performance number of 70, but his music takes him to 90, then what kind of damage or performance difficulties may occur before he gets back down to 70?

TOOLBOX

The Silence in Music

Look at the musical notes below and imagine that the notes represent all the hard work and preparation you do for competition. The notes express your physical movements and allow others to watch and enjoy your performances. The musical notes express you as an athlete.

Now, take one deep breath and allow your mind and emotions to focus on the blank space between the notes. Allow your mind and emotions to settle into the quiet background. Continue to breathe slowly and stay focused on the emptiness between each note. Notice how you have complete awareness of the notes without having to focus on the notes. You can trust your physical preparation by quieting your mind and emotions. Music makes no sense, and has no meaning, without the silence between the notes. When your mind and emotions are in the silence, your body can play the athletic notes. Focus your mind and emotions on the silence between the notes, so that your body can play the music…

The Athlete's Anthem

I am an athlete, my day has come. The moment I have been waiting for has arrived. The solutions I have been seeking are found. I am amazed at the life I have been given. It is good. I am peaceful, calm, confident, and complete just as I am. Nothing can add or take away from my individuality. All the illusions of fear and doubt have disappeared. I am complete just as I am... –Steve Hecht

Chapter Sixteen
Calm–Control–Attack

The less effort, the faster and more powerful you will be. –Bruce Lee

Calm-Control-Attack: Imagine a cheetah in the wild hunting for survival. Slow methodical positioning, a solid running posture, and then a sudden burst of speed is released as the cheetah attacks and devastates its prey.

Calm-Control-Attack: Imagine a bird of prey sitting high above an open prairie. The bird takes flight and silently swoops down on an unaware victim with patience and precision, the beauty of the flight and the effectiveness of the attack.

Calm-Control-Attack is the expression of all athletic movement in sports. It is the beginning, middle, and end of each athlete's performance, repeated over and over. *Calm-Control-Attack* is largely what sets athletes apart from one another. *Calm-Control-Attack* is a fundamental approach to athletic competition. Successful athletes and coaches understand the important connection between these three steps. They understand that neglecting one of these areas diminishes the others. Let's take a look at how these three operate together:

Calm: This is the mental and emotional foundation that every attack is built upon. This is the power plant of focus and energy, which allows an athlete to consistently provide control before he unleashes his attack. This is also the most overlooked aspect of training and coaching. A high performing athlete cannot sustain excellence if he does not learn to manage his mental and emotional approach–his *calm*.

In this book, the TOOLBOX and The Athlete's Anthem provide easy ways for athletes and coaches to incorporate mastery of the *calm* into their routines. Athletes and coaches can immediately experience the benefit of managing the *calm* before each training session or competition. The benefits of helping athletes and coaches experience *calm* lasts a lifetime.

Calm is built upon the following definition, and any break down in performance can be found in some part of this definition. In fact, after any sub-par performance an athlete or coach can read this definition and find where he missed the mark: The *calm* athlete is: **trusting, content, approved, he does not need or seek validation, he believes before he sees results, he knows what to do without over-thinking, he is powerful but not forceful, he is timely but does not rush, he achieves without indulging in achievement, he adjusts to the needs of the moment, he has singular focus and complete awareness, he does not resist what is, he accepts that everything is exactly the way it should be, he is creatively disciplined and entirely committed.**

Control: This is the physical mechanics of athletics and the main focus of most athletes and coaches. *Control*/mechanics are the primary basis for learning the physical movements of any sport. Athletes begin focusing on *control*/mechanics as soon as they begin playing a sport, and most athletes continue focusing on control until they are finished with their careers. The *control*/mechanical aspect of each sport has been written about tirelessly. There is *no doubt* that each sport has essential aspects for proper bio-mechanics; but no two players are alike, and there is no perfect way to run, throw a ball, swing a bat or golf club, etc. The *control*/mechanics may be taught similarly, but it is ultimately expressed differently in each athlete.

Unfortunately, too often athletes and coaches develop, or adopt their own idea of the best way to establish control simply through mechanics. They do this without any consideration for, or understanding of, its foundation, which is the *calm*. Even the casual sports fan can see *control*/mechanics break down during the pressure of competition. Yet, when an athlete struggles most coaches will watch video, or talk about how they need to continue working on their *control*/mechanics to improve. An athlete's breakdown in pressure situations is painted over with another conversation about *control*/mechanics. Why? Because most well-intentioned coaches have never understood or been trained how to deal with the *calm*. So, they continually return to what they know and are comfortable with, the mechanics of control.

In competition, emotional control is the overriding influence of any mechanical success or breakdown, yet, it is neglected largely by most coaches. Athletes know that they are capable of performing the mechanical movements, now if only their emotions could stay out of the way and let them.

Attack: This is the expression of calm and control working together. For athletes, successful attacks are applauded and rewarded. For coaches, wins and losses reflect the teaching and executing of successful attacks. For fans, successful attacks are why they keep coming back.

Most athletes have a natural tendency toward the attack. Coaches and parents teach the *control*/mechanics of the *attack* from an early age. The attack defines the sport, and it very often defines the athlete. In fact, nearly all coaching, training, and teaching centers around improving the *attack* by improving mechanics.

The athlete's attack is affected by many factors such as: size, strength, eyesight, nutrition, etc.; but none of these things can be greatly influenced once the competition begins. They are what they are.

The attack is the demonstration of how well *calm* and *control* are working in unison to achieve the goal. Whether the goal is throwing quality strikes, hitting the ball hard, catching the ball, shooting the ball, kicking, running, etc., the *attack* is the last thing that happens in an athlete's movement. If an athlete's *calm*, (performance number) is optimal; he can then effectively execute his *control* (mechanical training). Command of the *calm and control* yields a consistently lethal attack.

The Martial Arts understand, and are built upon, this *calm-control-attack* approach. However, unlike most athletes and coaches, martial artists dedicate much more time and attention to the *calm*, which they know is foundational for unleashing controlled and devastating attacks. True Martial Artists understand that the *attack* will take care of itself if the *calm and control* are given their proper attention. If you watch a beginning karate student, he is taught to breathe calmly and still his mind while he slowly perfects his forms. He is properly taught the *order* of successful attacks. I believe the next level of impact coaches in all sports will receive training in the *calm* in order to enhance athletic performances.

Picture yourself getting behind the wheel of your car to go on a long trip. The trip represents your athletic career. Your car is washed and waxed and looks great, but, as you drive along you look down at your gauges and notice none of them are working. You don't know how much fuel you have, you don't know if the engine is running too hot, you don't know how far you have gone, or how fast you are going. Then you get pulled over by a policeman who asks, "Do you know how fast you were going?" Of course, if you answer with an honest "No," you may receive an additional fine for operating a faulty vehicle. Let's look at some of the representations in this scenario:

1. The policeman is like a coach pulling an athlete aside to let him know he is going too fast or too slow.
2. The policeman is like a coach who can only judge what he sees on the outside, while he has no idea that the athlete's internal gauges are not working.
3. The policeman is like a coach who emotionally scolds a player for going too fast but is unwilling or unsure of how to fix his internal gauges.
4. The driver of the car is like an athlete who comes to rely on the tempo of the game, or other people, to pull him over and tell him he is going too fast. His internal gauges stopped working when he started relying too heavily on what his coaches thought or taught.
5. The driver of the car is like an athlete who is in a constant state of fear and anxiety because he is not sure if he has enough fuel to finish the trip. He doesn't know if he is running too hot, or whether he is going far enough or fast enough.

This simple illustration represents how so many athletes approach their careers. They don't know how fast they are going until the competition lets them know. The *calm* is neglected, the *control*/mechanics break down under pressure, and the *attack* is ineffective. ALL athletic movements are an expression of *calm-control-attack*. Which area are you covering or neglecting?

As another example, when the calm is neglected, the game seems like it is moving too fast. The control/mechanics break down and may cause:

1. A quarterback to miss defensive reads and not see all his open receivers.
2. A linebacker to miss a tackle or overrun a play.

3. A golfer to over-swing because he is still thinking about his last shot.
4. A pitcher to lose command of his pitches.
5. A hitter to expand the hitting zone and swing at balls.
6. A free throw shooter to lose his touch.

Calm represents the mental and emotional state of the athlete and provides the best connection for *control*/mechanics to work at their peak. If athletes and coaches neglect the *calm*, they partially neglect the *control*/mechanics that delivers the *attack*. *Calm* and *control* are the starting point for connecting the mind and the body; they are the bond that allows mind and body to work in unison. *Calm-control* is the basis for putting the athlete back in control of what he experiences during the *attack*. The athlete does NOT focus on getting *control*. Instead, he focuses on *calm* to have *control*. *Calm* allows the athlete to feel *control*, and together *calm-control* provides the foundation for a powerful *attack*.

TOOLBOX

A Walk on the Pier

This metaphor is used by a former National League All-Star. If he feels any tension or emotion get stuck in his chest or body during competition, he imagines that his walk to the on deck circle is like a walk onto a pier in the ocean. When he gets to the end of the pier (the on deck circle), he imagines big boulders on the pier that he gently pushes off into the ocean. He pictures the huge boulders as being like the emotion he is feeling in his chest. In his mind's eye, he sees these boulders sinking to the ocean floor as he feels the release from his chest. Over and over he lets the boulders sink to the ocean floor, as he feels the tension in his chest dissipate. He feels the calm, he feels the control, and he is prepared to unleash his attack.

The Athlete's Anthem

I let my mind, body, and emotions rest in the simplicity of silence; no straining, no striving, no resistance. I hear only silence, and I feel perfect stillness. As I uncover the silence and peace inside of me, I live and play in the freedom they provide. Fear, anxiety, and pressure do not exist in my silence. Silence and peace are at the core of all that I am. Every part of my performance is governed by the overwhelming silence and peace that exists inside of me. In this silence is where I find the true expression of my greatness. –Steve Hecht

Chapter Seventeen
Simplicity & Emotional Success

Difficulty comes when we try to make the simple –
complex. The more you really want something, the
more stress you create for yourself. Keep it simple.
–Unknown

Too much mechanical talk and thought robs an athlete of a necessary ingredient for athletic success – simplicity. Simplicity is not a feeling, but all athletes love the way it feels. The mind of an athlete gets short-circuited when a coach feels the need to communicate *all they know*. A quality at-bat should be simple. A quality golf swing should be simple. Athletes should be immersed in simplicity. Athletes and coaches that learn to value simplicity will have more creativity to deal with the challenges and complexities of sports and competition.

Let's look at the game of golf. The goal of golf is simple: hit the ball in the hole with as few swings as possible. The questions to ask yourself are: Can I achieve this goal better with more lessons, more equipment, and more information alone? Or, can I achieve this goal best with equal or more emphasis on simplicity and emotional success? Each year, golfers spend billions of dollars playing a game that leads them to the front door of *complexity*. They get lessons, hit countless golf balls, purchase books, videos, clubs, and gadgets in order to play better golf. All the while, they neglect the fact that their mental and emotional state is their biggest obstacle to playing well. Unfortunately, too often golfers surrender their emotional state to their score card, and they fail to recognize that mastering their emotions will consistently provide more enjoyment (absence of fear) and better scores. This is because their mental and emotional state frees their bodies to deliver the mechanical techniques that they already know with optimal results. Athletes and coaches find it easier, and more comfortable, to discuss the mechanics of a golfer's swing than the emotions that affect the swing. Simply stated, emotional swings break down the mechanics of golf swings.

As soon as the mind of a golfer begins to dwell on the importance of a golf shot or putt, he begins moving away from the dispassionate simplicity necessary for accuracy and consistency. Simplicity quiets the mind and allows it to focus, which lets a player trust his approach.

Simplicity lets a golfer trust himself and his swing. He can prepare and believe in his approach. ***The emotional success that a golfer demonstrates during a round of golf is the real indicator of his trust, preparation, and approach.*** Emotional displays during competition are revealing indicators of what an athlete or coach believes. The degree of trust a golfer has in himself and his golf swing is established by his emotional mastery. Emotional statements trump verbal statements. Try determining the success of a round of golf by the level of emotional mastery you have. How well your swing felt, and how well you scored will become a reflection of your emotional success, not the focus.

If you are a golfer, try this exercise in *simplicity* the next time you go to the driving range. First, remember 1 or 2 metaphors from the TOOLBOX. Second, instead of hitting a whole bucket of balls, set 10 golf balls aside for each club that you will swing. Third, before you hit each of those balls, focus only on letting go of all the emotion you feel. Remember, there is no time limit, no rush, no right or wrong, good or bad swing. Your goal is to release emotion before each swing. If you are in the habit of judging or criticizing yourself after each swing, let go of the emotion behind the judgment and criticism. Releasing emotion, releases energy stuck in the body. Hitting a golf ball is an exercise in moving and directing energy.

For example, try this ice cube metaphor: An ice cube is like your emotions in a frozen state. Your emotions should be fluid like water; but when feelings like fear, worry, nervousness, and anxiety are present, it causes those emotions to freeze up which creates tension. Like an ice cube melting, just allow yourself to melt away each emotion. Nervousness and anxiety are ice cubes that melt away. Continue melting away emotion before hitting each ball, and as you continue to release emotion, your mind will get quiet.

When you want approval, accolades, or recognition, you need to release these emotions, and each swing will lose its emotional charge and significance. When this happens, your emotions are no longer in charge, you are. You should notice you feel lighter and freer and have much less tension in your swing. Also, notice that you did not forget how to swing the club or hit the ball because you are able to trust your training and preparation without thought. *Enjoy yourself.*

Could you allow yourself to feel this way for an entire round of golf? Let your emotions go, and then take the swing. Let your emotions go, and then take the swing – over and over. Walking or riding from shot-to-shot becomes an exercise in releasing emotion and not thinking about the mechanics of the shot. Do not judge your previous swing or be anxious about the next one. Focus on letting all of your overexcitement, anxiety, or fear go each moment of the round. When you are playing with quiet

123

power, you will not get rattled by a poor shot or overeager by a quality shot. Emotional success is consistent and does not get worked up by good or bad shots. When you are too emotionally invested in a shot, it's like a withdrawal from focus and concentration.

No emotion, know peace. Swing after swing is an expression of emotional mastery and nothing else. An athlete who learns to compete with emotional success is best positioned for more consistently maximizing his potential. It teaches simplicity and trust from the inside out. Emotional success is the best tool a golfer or athlete can take into training or competition. A golfer can compete with emotional success, or he can compete with mechanical thought, but, I believe that emotional mastery is the most insightful instructor an athlete can have, especially in competition. It provides focus for the current golf shot, whereas mechanical thought is focused on the past shot and the upcoming shot. When your emotions are freely moving and being released, your mind is quiet, your body is relieved of excess tension, and you experience emotional success.

What situations can occur on a golf course that will make you retreat to the familiar *safety* of mechanical thought? Is it a shank, slice, 3-putt, etc.? When these situations occur, what emotion is behind them? If you let go of the emotion behind the poor shot or putt, you will lessen the likelihood of it occurring again; but if you keep the emotion associated with the shot or situation, you will increase the chances of it reoccurring.

Let's look at a 3-putt. If you think about 3-putting you will notice that there is emotion behind the thought. If you keep the emotion, you will keep the thought. Remember, emotion means energy-in-motion. The moment an emotion is suppressed it looks for some way to escape. Thought provides a means for escape. The more emotion that fuels the thoughts behind a 3-putt, the more likely it is to occur. When you let go of the emotion behind a 3-putt, you will decrease the likelihood of it happening again.

The Golfer's Cycle of Insanity

The great game of golf is fun, healthy, and exciting for those who play and enjoy watching it. Ironically, the emotional enthusiasm of playing a round of golf is the first major hurdle for many golfers to overcome. Golfers love the anticipation and excitement that comes with playing a round of golf, but they fail to recognize that these powerful feelings may be their biggest obstacle to playing at their best. All of that emotion and enthusiasm is carried to the first tee box, and the emotional spike can be so high that it takes several holes, or even the whole round, before the emotion wears off enough to fully focus and flow in the round. Sometimes a golfer gets off to a good start, and sometimes he can't find the center of the golf club. He may make a few good shots, and then lose his cool and composure with a few poor shots. Again, emotional swings affect golf swings.

Golfers and athletes that feed on the addictive feeling of excessive excitement make it more difficult to achieve peak performances and consistency. Too much enthusiasm can be like the food you love to eat, but you know is not good for you. When you curb the overflow of excitement and experience more peace and control, you will have more focus and play at a higher level with more consistency. Excessive enthusiasm requires an enormous amount of energy to manage and maintain, so allow yourself to experience that excitement when the competition is over. You will see more consistent and predictable results. Emotional success means that you are able to regulate your energy. *Emotional success is like a powerful log of slow burning happiness and contentment, while emotional excitement is a quick fix of jittery black coffee.*

TOOLBOX

Getting Back Into Rhythm

This simple yet powerful technique comes from Ilchi Lee's book *Brain Wave Vibration*. This method helps to quiet thoughts created in the brain (neocortex) that cause the body stress. It returns control of your brain to the genius of the brain stem. The brain stem controls breathing, heart rate, stress response and many other autonomic functions. This is a way to slow your mind down and a very effective method to sleep better. Try it for 5-10 minutes before lying down to sleep. Many athletes have reported immediately sleeping better with this technique.

Now, simply sit down somewhere, take a deep breath, shut your eyes, and *slowly* move your head from left to right for two minutes. Just slowly move your head comfortably to the left, and then comfortably to the right. *Do this slowly*, then open your eyes and notice the difference. You can do this for two minutes, or as long you like.

The Athlete's Anthem

Fear and anxiety cover up the power of peace for performance. Uncovering and constantly experiencing peace brings power to my life as an athlete. Peace is a direct reflection of the confidence and trust that I have in my abilities. *Peace is NOT passive in sports. Instead, it is powerful, fearless and devastating to any opponent.* Peace provides the foundation for me to withstand the ups and downs of competition. Peace reveals the weapons in my arsenal. I do not have to compete for peace, I accept it. Peace will compete for me. It is my expression of quiet power. –Steve Hecht

Chapter Eighteen

The Power of Exchange

There's no use talking about the problem unless you talk about the solution. –Betty Williams

Words have meaning and power. They create emotion and carry emotion. As I have previously emphasized, emotion is energy-in-motion. Words are spoken thoughts, and when "power words" are spoken with conviction, they release power. Powerful, positive words elevate feelings and are like nutrition for an athlete's mind and emotions, while negative words are like junk food for an athlete's mind and emotions. Negative words can fill a void, but they have little energy or life.

To illustrate, have you ever entered a room or environment where people were speaking poorly of you? There is a tangible feeling that you can sense as you encounter the sudden silence. In the same way, have you ever entered a room where people were speaking well of you? There is also a feeling that can be sensed rather easily. Words carry energy and emotion. Powerful, positive words energize the body and calm the emotions. They can lead to peace and produce commanding results.

Question: Can a high energy football player be at peace mentally and emotionally and perform at a high level?

Answer: Yes. If a football player plays best at a performance number of 90, this means his mental and emotional intensity needs to be high in order for his body to perform best. This does NOT mean he is not at peace. *Peace is not passive.* Peace wisely recognizes and regulates how much mental and emotional energy it takes for an athlete to perform at his peak, regardless of the sport he plays. Words and metaphors help athletes arrive at their performance number with less effort. When an athlete or coach rests in peace, he wisely knows when to be a lion or a lamb. Athletes or coaches who do not recognize the difference create their own difficulties.

The power of exchanging words and emotions is a principle that all athletes and coaches can benefit from. This principle recognizes that simply wanting to get rid of a thought or an emotion does not work, unless it is exchanged for another thought or emotion. Unwanted thoughts and feelings must be exchanged for more powerful and productive thoughts and feelings.

Successful athletes and coaches use the power of exchanging words and emotions to eliminate negativity and worthless mind chatter. Less productive thoughts and emotions, like fear, are replaced with more constructive thoughts like courage. Emotions reflect and encourage thoughts. Productive thoughts promote productive emotions; likewise, an absence of emotion results in an absence of thought. Words that are positive and powerful are like rungs on an athlete's ladder that lead to elevated thought and emotion. You cannot arrive at the top rung of a ladder until you have stepped onto the lower rungs. Each time you compete from a higher rung on the ladder, you increase your chances for performance success.

When elevated thoughts replace inferior thoughts, the inferior thoughts disappear because two thoughts cannot coexist. Some lower forms of thoughts for athletes and coaches are: thinking about mechanics, wanting to prove yourself, wanting others to think well of you and your abilities, seeking appreciation, or seeking praise. These are the types of thoughts that prevent athletes and coaches from reaching the pinnacle of performance where purpose, power, and peace reside.

Positive statements, metaphors, and power words enhance the mind and emotions of athletes and coaches. Power words are an expression of an athlete's nature. Athletes naturally gravitate toward words that validate their greatness. Power words have a maximum impact on an athlete's mind and emotions, because power is unleashed when the mind is given clear purpose and well-defined focus.

It stands to reason that if confidence is constructive then fear is destructive. Fear is at the bottom of an athlete's performance ladder, and peace is at the top. Unproductive emotions come from unproductive thoughts, and empowering emotions come from empowering thoughts. Low is exchanged for high, and unproductive is exchanged for productive.

The following words contain energy, power, and emotion. Allow yourself to feel the emotion behind each word. As you read the words, speak them out loud and notice the feeling that is created inside of you. Interestingly, current research has discovered a region in the brain that responds only to the human voice. This area of the brain is not activated by any other sound. Let the emotion freely flow through you. Take the feeling in and immediately let it go. Understand that even one word can quiet your mind and free your emotions. Different words will have different feelings at different times, according to your current needs:

POWER WORDS

All-powerful, remarkable, dynamic, energetic, vitality, astonishing, swift, confident, focused, blissful, priceless, gratified, high-minded, cool-headed, imaginative, unyielding, super-colossal, almighty, impelling, disciplined, versatile, brilliant, undisturbed, imposing, genius, strength, certain, intelligent, level-headed, magnificent, exemplary, bold, marvelous, swift, creative, unhurried, masterful, esteemed, beautiful, mighty, mind-blowing, stately, noble, outstanding, regal, peaceful, clearheaded, poised, at peace, explosive, potent, dominating, powerhouse, anchored, precise, monumental, awe-inspiring, uncompromising, superior, transcendent, incomparable, preeminent, celestial, immovable, at ease, purposeful, radiant, exceptional, renowned, majestic, exquisite, resilient, imperial, lofty, serene, harmonious, inspired, spirited, content, breathtaking, eternal, genuine, superb, authentic, committed, excellent, supreme, tenacious, firm, tranquil, distinctive, extravagant, definite, authoritative, tremendous, courageous, exalted, commanding, unflappable, elevated, assured, unmoved, fearless, illustrious, untroubled, established, glorious, vast, composed.

TOOLBOX

The Quiet Mind

What does an athlete's mind look like when it is quiet? When an athlete identifies and experiences any number of the feelings listed below, he is moving toward or experiencing a *quiet mind*. Spend a few moments slowly reading over each word. Notice what feeling each word creates in you, and let the emotion of that word freely flow through you.

Ageless, Creative, Sharp, Vigorous, Open, Enthusiastic, Positive, Intuitive, Assured, Dynamic, Optimistic, Motivated, Strong, Perfected, Non-Resistant, Still, Boundless, Calm, Tranquil, Cheerful, Resilient, Decisive, Elated, Appreciative, Focused, Aware, Free, Centered, Friendly, Glowing, Humorous, Light, Mellow, Nothing to Change, Eternal, One, Purposeful, Responsive, Secure, Fulfilled, Spontaneous, Pure, Considerate, Quiet, Serene, Clear, Supportive, Timeless, Confident, Alert, Tireless, Understanding, Belonging, Unlimited, Certain, Envisioned, Well, Complete, Whole.

The Athlete's Anthem

When I elevate my thoughts and emotions, I find that it is much easier to focus on the task-at-hand. Affirming and constructive thoughts and emotions elevate me, and help me rise above the heavy burden of my ego.

I imagine that each game or performance is like someone giving me tickets to go to my favorite vacation spot. It may be lying on a beach in Hawaii, sleeping in a cabin in the mountains, or having breakfast at a castle in Ireland. I _do_ _not_ need to get two hits, pitch a shut-out, or have the game winning RBI in order to go on this vacation. Win or lose, I will receive the tickets at the end of the game. The only stipulation is that I mentally and emotionally focus on the beauty of where I am going, while I am physically committed to the competition. I go all in. I focus on how it will feel to be there, how it will smell, what colors I will see, who I will be with, and what things I want to see and do, etc.

Each time my mind tries to distract my focus from the vacation (the moment), I think about some other characteristic of the trip or location. I direct my thoughts and emotions toward this trip, and when the game begins I am mentally and emotionally free. –Steve Hecht

Chapter Nineteen

The Coach's Corner

I've learned that people will forget what you said, people will forget what you did, but people will never forget how you made them feel.

-Maya Angelou

Coaches, there are three primary ways that you communicate to players:

1) Your body language
2) Your tone of voice
3) The content of your words

It is unreasonable to expect players to perform from the penthouse if you consistently communicate to them from the basement. Calm, confident, and trusting athletes do not often come from anxious, fearful, and distrusting coaches. Our assignment as coaches is to provide an environment where players can maximize their athletic potential. We must help players peel back the layers of mental and emotional unrest that hinder their performances. All players want something different, but ultimately, they all want to feel at ease and at peace. They want to know that they are enough as a person even if they fall short as a performer. The more that a player's value is connected to his performance, the more performance anxiety he experiences. Players have difficulty when they want one or more of the following:

1) Acceptance, approval, and/or appreciation.
2) Command and/or control.
3) Safety and/or security.

Some players need more or less, but underperforming athletes are striving for one, or all, of these things. Give them what they need until they learn to believe in themselves. Teach players to believe and trust before competition so that they believe and trust during competition. Help them to get out of their own way. Emotionally successful coaches are predictable and consistent. Players enjoy the environment created by a positive, predictable, and consistent coach. Emotions are the most powerful characteristic of our nature, and they can be the most constructive, or destructive aspect of an athlete's career and life. A coach may be enthusiastically positive or damagingly negative.

Moods may vary according to wins and losses, or batting average and ERA. Impact coaches are predictably consistent. Even when an impact coach is spontaneously emotional, he is most often constructive. The impact coach consistently communicates trust and confidence through predictability and consistency. Trust and confidence are a natural outflow of the emotionally successful coach. The unpredictable coach breaks down a player's trust, and the inconsistent coach breaks down confidence. Whether you are raising children or developing athletes, predictability and consistency are the currencies that produce trust and confidence. Predictability and consistency provide an environment for players to believe in themselves. Coaches who have learned to manipulate and motivate players through moodiness and inconsistency are resented. These types of coaches drain the energy of players, and ultimately they center the team and its success on themselves. They make themselves the focus, and this makes it more difficult for the team to maintain focus and capture their own identity. Players unknowingly use an extraordinary amount of energy seeking approval or staying in the coach's good graces, which leaves less energy for them to focus on their performance. Pleasing the coach then becomes the player's goal, while he *hopes* to succeed during competition and reach the goal.

An impact coach is relentless in his efforts to empower players. He is constantly positioning himself to lead his team through *service*. The less a coach makes himself the center of attention, the easier it is for the team to find its personality. A coach recognizes his position, power, and authority. An *impact* coach recognizes his position to guide and senses a mandate to encourage with his power and authority. He understands that the cycle of a healthy and successful team begins with him empowering and allowing players to be themselves. The impact coach knows his team's ongoing success depends on his ability to connect with, and embolden players to maximize their potential.

Below are a few different coaching methods that I have learned, used, or developed. Adapt any of them for your players, sport, or coaching style.

1) Schedule a "silent bullpen" for your pitchers: A pitcher's routine is sometimes filled with anxiety and stress, so create a day that they can look forward to throwing without it. Schedule practice sessions that are performed without verbal coaching or talking. For example, I once worked with a 1st round draft pick that was having

difficulty commanding his pitches and being consistent. He was at the AAA level and was very anxious about his outings. His scheduled bullpen was the next day, and we agreed to throw the bullpen in silence. The only assignment he had during the bullpen was to let go of any emotion, judgment, or criticism after each pitch. No matter where the ball went out of his hand, he committed to releasing emotion and letting the bullpen reflect his emotional control. At the end of the bullpen, he calmly handed me the ball, and we slowly walked over to the bench and sat down. After a few moments of silence he said, "That was the most fun I've had throwing a bullpen since becoming a professional." Some weeks later, I was in the Major League locker-room when he walked in for the first time. He said his new found success began with the *silent bullpen*. His confidence and trust were found in silence. An athlete should not perform to find peace.

2) Ask a player which question describes him best:
   a) Does this game make you who you are?
   b) Does this game reveal who you are? Or,
   c) Does this game conceal who you are?

These questions very often create different reactions and emotions from players. They sometimes allow players to see themselves in a different light and encourage them to reevaluate their approach to competition. Does your coaching style encourage players to be who they are, help reveal to themselves who they really are, or conceal their potential?

3) Ask players to identify any person, place, or situation that causes them to spike emotionally. Very often players are unaware, or unsure, of what to do about emotional spikes in competition. Some examples I hear

quite often: a coach or parent yelling, an umpire missing a call, making an error, striking out, hitting with two strikes, not feeling 100%, feeling too strong, etc. Any number of factors can cause a player to spike emotionally, but the methods in the TOOLBOX will allow a player to defuse these situations before they disrupt his performance. The effects of emotional spikes are minimized by releasing the emotion behind the person, place, or situation that causes them.

4) Move at 50% speed and effort. When an athlete gets out of rhythm and timing physically, it is very beneficial to go through drills or movements more slowly. Too often athletes feel rushed to get through drills, or are rushed during a game and lose feel and focus. If you slow them down on purpose, it is a good way to get them back on track. When the player uses a TOOLBOX method with less effort, he captures his natural rhythm and timing more easily.

5) Engage in "dry work" on a regular basis. Pitchers cannot physically throw as often as hitters swing a bat, but dry work allows both of them to be productive. Effective dry work consists of a player going through his physical movements at game speed while releasing thought and emotion in between each repetition. Going through physical repetitions is beneficial, but releasing emotion and thought brings value similar to relaxation and visualization. Overall, I have experienced much less resistance from athletes performing dry work, than trying to get them to engage in relaxation and visualization techniques. There is always more value in implementing a technique that is used more regularly without resistance.

6) Humor, fun, and enjoyment are very powerful and positive ways of elevating a player's emotional levels. I had the great pleasure of watching how Ken Griffey Jr. used humor to positively affect the team and clubhouse in Seattle. Humor and enjoyment helped pull the team together and maintain consistency during a long season of ups and downs. Humor and enjoyment, combined with focus, have a very positive impact on players and teams. Yet, humor and enjoyment without focus is misery. The more that emotion flows naturally, the more humor, fun, and enjoyment is experienced.

7) To help an athlete quiet his thoughts and emotions, have him write down every role he identifies with. For example: I am an athlete, I am a student, I am a son, I am a friend, I am a father, I am a husband, etc. Then after each role have him ask himself this question:

And what if I am more than that?

Keep asking this question until all the roles you play are exhausted. He will notice how his thoughts quiet down, and emotions get calm.

8) Stop trying to figure everything out. Playing sports is not a *problem*. Over-thinking keeps an athlete in a mode of desperation and survival. Stop searching for answers and start letting go of the emotions behind the questions. Let emotion go and give your mind a break. Set it free from the burden of having to figure anything out. The more you think about resolving an issue, the greater the issue becomes. When you let go of the emotion that comes from the issue, the more creative you will become at

resolving the issue. A calm mind and steady emotions attract solutions with less effort. Athletes must learn that their minds and emotions are most creative and insightful during periods of quiet and inner stillness. Like trying too hard to remember someone's name you once knew, walk away and let it come to you.

9) If an athlete is having difficulty with a particular skill, determine the desired outcome and ask the athlete to show you how to accomplish it. For example, a first baseman was trying to get comfortable with his footwork, and was told the "right" way to order his steps. He continued to struggle getting it right because he was caught up in mechanical thought. So, after much frustration, he and I went to an empty field and instead of talking about the mechanics of his steps, I asked him where he wanted to end up when the ball was pitched. I drew a line in the dirt and then asked him how an athlete would get to that line. His steps worked smoothly, and he was freed from the prison created by thought. After all, it didn't really matter if he started with his left foot or right foot, as long as he got to the spot.

10) If you want to know if a player's worth is connected to his performance, then ask him if he can give himself feelings of approval for no reason whatsoever. Just ask him to sit there and give himself waves of approval without doing anything to earn them. You will be surprised how difficult it is for players to give themselves approval without having a reason. The more a player finds satisfaction in results, the further he gets from the pinnacle of peace and quiet power. The more a coach or player finds satisfaction in the person he is, the easier it is to compete and maximize his performance

potential. Success is all too often attached to the burden and pain of results. For a coach or athlete, what else is there? He knows pleasure from winning, or pain from losing. Learn to give yourself approval for no reason at all. This will allow you to tap into the quiet power of peace to find emotional success. *Now* an athlete can maximize his performance potential.

Putting on My Uniform

I will never put my uniform on the same way again. My uniform is a symbol of my authority. The authority I have been given to express my greatness. My uniform is the vehicle that reveals my unique gifts, talents, and abilities. My uniform is not made of cloth, it is made of passion. Beneath my uniform lie passion and a deeply confident peace. My peace is the basis for my power. I have the power that brings this uniform to life... I have the passionate peace that empowers this uniform to express my greatness... My greatness comes to life the moment I put this uniform on... –Steve Hecht

TOOLBOX

Drop the Ball of Emotion

Imagine holding a ball in your hand that represents an emotion that you want to let go of. Imagine the emotion is anger, and you feel constricted by it. Imagine squeezing the ball of anger as hard as you can and then slowly opening your hand and dropping it off the edge of the Grand Canyon. Just relax your hand and watch the ball of anger fall into the Colorado River below and get washed away. Drop as many balls of emotion into the river below until you feel lighter and unburdened...

The Athlete's Anthem

The Beauty of Competition

The Beauty of Competition will briefly embrace victories and let go of crushing defeats. The Beauty of Competition is like a coin with two sides. One side is planned, prepared, and predictable; and the other is unplanned, unprepared, and unpredictable. Neither side of the coin consumes me. I have stood in the circle of victory, and I have stared down defeat.

If I choose to remain safe, and stand outside the fire of competition, I will NEVER lose, and I will NEVER know the thrill and enjoyment of victory. I will be safe, but I will be unfulfilled. My body may be present, but unless my heart and mind go all in, I will not know the beauty of competition.

The Beauty of Competition is like a mirror that reveals me to myself. Each time I compete, I see another part of myself, and my greatness is reflected. –Steve Hecht

Services Offered

PINNACLE PERFORMANCE TRAINING CAMP:
An in-depth and interactive training course customized for coaches and/or athletes that need a powerful edge in training and competition. These simple, yet profound techniques and insights will help coaches and athletes improve their performance immediately. Whatever your sport may be, Training Camp will bring fresh insight to the way you train, play, and coach. Typical length is 3-6 hours.

PINNACLE WORKSHOPS: These workshops are highly specific and compelling. Each workshop is 60-90 minutes, and includes a practical question and answer session. For a list of workshops, please visit thehechteffect.com.

NEXT LEVEL SEMINARS: These intensely focused seminars last 3-4 hours and are specifically designed for learning a competition mindset. The seminar is fast paced, concentrated, and most of all experiential. Coaches and athletes will *feel* what works for competition. They will learn how to elevate their mindset for pinnacle performances. The information and experience is powerful, and will have a lasting impact. Athletes and coaches will be fully equipped with information to immediately implement these tools and techniques.

CORPORATE PERFORMANCE TRAINING: This training program is uniquely designed to provide organizations with insights and methods that have been proven to enhance performance. Corporate performance training is informative and entertaining, while providing immediate occupational application. Performance training will have a lasting impact on your organization.

CHURCH AND NON-PROFIT: Principle based training for those involved in the service to others. With an emphasis to provide a new approach to old problems, each participant will receive insight, tools, and techniques for improving the manner in which they help and serve. Volunteers and staff need to be refreshed, and they will have fun learning new ways to give and receive help.

KEYNOTE SPEAKER: Steve Hecht's career as a professional athlete and Major League coach has allowed him to work with some of the best athletes in the world. He shares his impacting stories and methods for improving performance and life. His simple yet innovative perspective will change the way you view sports and life. You will walk away challenged, entertained, and motivated.

For more information, please go to:
thehechteffect.com
Or contact Steve at: **steve@thehechteffect.com**